R H Y M E S
O F   A
W E S T E R N
L O G G E R

Spar Tree

Photo by Leonard Frank, courtesy Jewish Historical Society of BC

RHYMES
OF A
WESTERN
LOGGER

The Collected Poems of Robert Swanson

WITH A FOREWORD BY
HOWARD WHITE

HARBOUR PUBLISHING

HARBOUR PUBLISHING
P.O. Box 219
Madeira Park, BC Canada V0N 2H0

Cover design by Roger Handling
Cover painting by Bus Griffiths, photographed by Bob Cain
Author photograph by Stephen Osborne
Published with the assistance of the Canada Council and the
British Columbia Cultural Services Branch.
Printed and bound in Canada by Friesen Printers

Book 1: *Rhymes of a Western Logger* copyright © 1942 by R.E.
Swanson, originally published by The Lumberman Printing Co.
Ltd., Vancouver.
Book 2: *Rhymes of a Lumberjack* copyright © 1943 by Robert E.
Swanson, originally published by Thomas Allen, Limited,
Toronto. Illustrations by Bert Bushell.
Book 3: *Bunkhouse Ballads* copyright © 1945 by Robert E.
Swanson, originally published by Thomas Allen, Limited,
Toronto. Illustrations by Bert Bushell.
Book 4: *Rhymes of a Haywire Hooker* copyright © 1953 by Robert
E. Swanson and "Seattle Red", originally published by The
Lumberman Printing Co. Ltd., Vancouver. Only poems by
Robert E. Swanson are included in this edition.

Canadian Cataloguing in Publication Data
Swanson, Robert E.
Rhymes of a western logger.
ISBN 1-55017-066-X
I. Title
PS8537.W34A17 1992   C811'.54   C92-091161-7
PR9199.3.S92A17 1992

C O N T E N T S

Book 4: RHYMES OF A HAYWIRE HOOKER

Before the "Great Cut" began

THE POETRY OF ROBERT SWANSON

Howard White

THE EASIEST WAY to describe Robert Swanson's writing is to say he did for the loggers of the BC coast what Robert Service did for the goldminers of the Klondike. When I was a kid growing up in my dad's logging camp during the 1950s, a signed copy of Service's *Songs of a Sourdough* was one of the more thumbworn volumes in our narrow cookhouse bookshelf, but in popularity terms it was a long way back of the little Swanson chapbooks *Rhymes of a Western Logger, Rhymes of a Lumberjack, Bunkhouse Ballads* and *Rhymes of a Haywire Hooker*, which were never idle long enough to get put up on the bookshelf at all, and soon began making the rounds of the bunkhouses, never to be seen again in one piece.

Swanson never hit the international bigtime like Service and never had the opportunity of retiring to the French Riviera on his royalties if he'd wanted to—which he wouldn't have—but in the world of the BC coast logger, he achieved legendary status, a status he retains to this day among that dwindling company of snaggle-toothed veterans who were there. By Swanson's own count his four little books sold eighty-two thousand copies, and at their peak in the forties and fifties held a place in coastal bunkhouses from Aberdeen to Sandspit as standard reading material alongside *True*,

Argosy, and *The Hi-Baller.* Mostly they were distributed by the old Harry Smith News Agency, and Swanson wants it known that he never stooped to the actual selling of books himself, and most especially never recited for free drinks in beer parlours (although plenty of other people did this on his behalf). Nevertheless, he took an active interest in marketing matters, purposely designing the chapbooks narrow enough to fit the *Reader's Digest* racks found in every skid road smokeshop and camp commissary, but tall enough to stick up where every passing chokerman would spot them.

In this manner Swanson's words became part of every logger's world, and the phrases Swanson dreamed up to describe the trials and joys of the logger's daily round were quickly absorbed into the everyday parlance of the working bush ape. in the sixties when I found myself back in the camps as an active participant it was still common to hear men on the job quoting a stanza or two from "The Ambitious Whistle Punk" or "The Cat Skinner's Prayer" to illuminate particularly snarly situations or bolster unlikely arguments. Nor was it uncommon during Saturday bull sessions in the bunkhouse or the Minstrel pub to see some knotty old faller lean back in his bar chair and beller out the full text of "The Death of Rough House Pete" or "The Worthy Bed Bug," accepting the free rounds that followed with grave condescension.

Robert Eugene Swanson (his bricklayer father named him simply "Bob" but the son elaborated on it later himself) was born in England before the first war, but when his parents shipped out to Vancouver Island during Bob's infancy, Bob decided to go along. That's an old line, but in Bob's case it's not far off true. He was born precocious. As a young boy in East Wellington he played hookey so he could ride the local logging train, and by fourteen he was confident enough around camp to quit school and go to work full time. By seventeen he had his third class steam engineer's papers and a few years later he upgraded to first class. He spent the shutdowns in Vancouver with all the other bush apes, but instead of blowing his stake on the skid road in the company of Rough House Pete, Johnnie-on-the-Spot, Seattle Red and the other rangitangs he would later record in his verse, he took courses

from private tutors and eventually earned a professional engineer-
ing degree—without ever having attended a university.

In 1936 Swanson jumped from the logging camp circuit to
government service as boiler inspector, and later, Chief Railway
Inspector and safety inspector as well, roles in which he probably
did more to make BC's woods safe than any other person. When
trucks came into use and companies couldn't find a fail-safe air
braking system, Swanson invented one himself, and lived to see it
adopted as the standard all over North America. When the new
diesel locomotives started creating mayhem at highway crossings
because motorists didn't recognize their newfangled monotone
horns as the sound of an approaching train, Swanson drew on his
childhood love of train sounds to devise a tuned hexatone air horn
assembly that re-created the sad familiar wail of the steam train
whistle—and made the crossings safe once again. That invention
too, he lived to see copied all over the industrialized world, to the
point he was able to establish himself in private business manufac-
turing tuned whistle systems when he retired from government
service. It was Swanson whom Prime Minister Lester Pearson
called upon to fit the Centennial train with a whistle that played
O Canada for the country's hundredth birthday in 1967, and whose
handiwork is familiar to thousands of Vancouver residents hearing
that same patriotic blast from the top of the BC Hydro building
every day at 12 o'clock noon.

Given his renaissance-style versatility, it isn't hard to imagine
the young Swanson waking up one day with the idea he could lick
the odds at writing the same way he had at logging and book
larnin'. The example of Robert Service here is more than just a
literary reference. It was Service and the immense popularity of his
Klondike balladeering Swanson credits with triggering his interest
in writing, and his first attempts were verses about the north—
which he'd never visited. He sent some of these efforts to Service,
and later met the successful writer at the Vancouver book store
owned by Service's brother. Service encouraged Swanson, but
advised him to butt out of the north and write about the wild world
of the westcoast logger, which nobody else was doing. It was good
advice.

11

Swanson's first three books are reprinted here unchanged from their original form, except for a bit of minor copy editing. The fourth book, *Rhymes of a Haywire Hooker*, was largely a collection of poems by other loggers including his older brother Dan (A.K.A. Seattle Red), so we have included only those few which were actually written by Swanson himself. In addition, we have added several poems which didn't appear in any previous books.

Like Service's writing, Swanson's has a breath of authenticity, a spirit of workplace vitality, which lifts it above the common run of folk verse. As such it makes an important contribution to the story of the west coast, and it is high time it was available to contemporary readers in one convenient volume.

BOOK I:

RHYMES
OF A
WESTERN
LOGGER

WARNING

This book of verse — it might be worse,
And still it might be better.
A logger's ways is all it says,
Dead true — right to the letter.

I don't profess to just say "yes"
And write as is convention.
To shock the prudes and holy dudes
Is more like my intention.

I might offend a pious friend
By truths which here are written.
But truth is truth, although uncouth;
With such my pen is smitten.

THE CALL OF THE TALL TIMBERS

There's a life that is close unto nature, where the soul is happy
    and free,
And you live by the brawn of your muscle—ah, there is the life
    to suit me:
Where the air is fragrant with perfume of the pines and the
    mountains high.
Oh god! if I stay in the city, I feel I am going to die.

Way out where the timber is godly—hundreds of feet in the air!
Reaching their limbs to the heavens, striving for sunlight, a
    share—
Where the brooklet springs from the mountain like tears from a
    weeping God,
But pure and clear as a crystal, through the forest's root-tangled
    sod:
Where the bluffs, they are bold and daring in defiance of
    gravity's law;
Where the stillness of slumbering canyon is awakened by
    tree-falling saw.

A saw in the hand of a logger, with rippling muscles of brawn,
As he thrills to the holler of "Timber-r-r," and the monarch falls
    dizzily on—
To crush in its falling the younger, "side winders" crash noisily
    down,
And the air is alive with the branches that were draped as her
    sylvan gown.
The "bucker" with saw, axe and hammer, his wedges and bottle
    of oil,
Will butcher the monarch in log lengths, by the sweat of his
    brow and his toil.
The glistening ribbons of "chokers," in the hand of a fast "rigging
    crew,"

Will whisk the monarch to "spar tree," 'midst snorting and
    hull-a-baloo,
And steel-fingered "tongs" of the loaders, when handled with
    dexterous skill,
Will send the monarch a-rolling on cars to the hideous mill.

O! Could I stand on the side-hill, where echoes the rigging
    crew's call,
Or to crouch on the brow of a canyon, that's brimful of
    thundering brawl;
Or to float on the "boom" as they're dumping and witness the
    spume and the spray
As the logs tumble off in the salt-chuck and the booms are
    floated away:
Or I wish I could stand on a "brow-log" and gawk at the rigger on
    high,
'Till my eyes are watered and smarting by gazing so long at the
    sky,
And I'm pining to sit on a "speeder," a "locie," or car on the
    track,
For the call of the camp is within me, it's throbbing and calling
    me back.

When the twig in the brush is the driest, and needles of fir taint
    the air,
Humidity drops to its lowest, it's then that I want to be there.
When a column of smoke rises skyward, and terror it strikes in
    the heart!
And the forest fire's doing its damndest, with every one playing
    his part!
It sounds like a thousand machine guns, a roar, and a tumult and
    cry,
As the crown fire sweeps to the heavens and the floating
    incendiaries fly.
It reminds you of Hell-fire and brimstone, and your eyes are
    a-burning with smoke,

As the wind whips it up to a fury, like the Devil is playing his
    joke:
But you never give up 'till it's conquered, you fight with the
    demon to quell.
It's tough! and I can't say I like it; but it beats this life all to Hell.

O! Could I stand in the valley, that's "trembling" with summery
    heat,
Where the logs lay "bucked" oh the side-hill, in lengths to a
    hundred odd feet;
There's Cedar and Fir, and there's Hemlock, that's eight or nine
    feet on the stump,
That will thunder and crash over windfalls, and land at the
    "tree" with a thump:
And I'm longing again for the bunkhouse, with my packsack
    over my bunk,
I could dream of a trip to the city, and maybe enjoy a good
    drunk.
This job in a shipyard is lousy—a paradise fit for a tramp.
So to Hell with a life in the city; I'm off—to a logging camp!

THE LOGGER'S SWEETHEART

She stalks the street, her prey to meet, that she may dine and drink;
Through hennaed hair, to hide despair, she gives her beckoning wink:
With slinking bluff she totes her stuff on the blazing skid roads of sin
And with fond good-byes and tears in her eyes she looks for another to
skin.

* * * *

This is a tale of the passion-lust trail of a logger who came into
town
With a roll of "dough" he was bound to blow, his passion and
thirst to drown.
While making the trip on the town-bound ship, at poker he'd
won quite a stake,
And now he was sure he'd find him a girl that loved just for
loving's sake.
As he came into town, with his packsack brown, caulk boots
tied on by the laces—
He remembered his dreams and passionate schemes, and
thoughts of voluptuous faces.

Like a pending groom, he hired him a room in the finest join of
the town,
And he signed on the card, like a scribbling bard, 'ere he tossed
his packsack down.
That hotel clerk was a queer-looking "jerk," with hairs on his
upper lip;
Like the misplaced brow, from the eye of a sow, and a hand with
a "dead-fish grip."
He looked like a simp, or maybe a pimp, but he said to the
logger gent:
"So you're Pannicky Bill of the brush and hill, I can see you're on
pleasure bent."
Bill handed his roll, like a trusting soul, to be placed in the iron
vault,

So when he was bold, he couldn't be rolled—if he was—well, it
    wasn't his fault.
With a six-bit tip to the "hair-decked lip" he was whisked on
    high to his floor,
And the "hop" took his grip, stood there for the tip, with his
    hand on the numbered door!

He climbed in the tub, and began to scrub the grime of the
    woods from his skin;
He had ordered a "crock," and, hearing a knock, he hollered,
    "Come on right in!
Put her there on the bunk, with the rest of the junk, and bring
    up some glasses and ice;
You seem like a sport that might be the sort to give to a
    man—advice.
When I'm clean and neat, I would like to meet a dame of my
    heart's desire!
A little blond 'beaut,' that's awfully cute—O boy, the things I
    would buy 'er!"
So with soap in his eyes, O what a surprise, was there sat right
    on the bed!
The girl of his dreams and fanciful schemes—blond hair
    (inclined to be red).
Her eyes were blue as the twilight dew, her cheeks "like the
    bloom of the rose."
And her features bland, like a sculptor's hand, had chiselled that
    perfect nose.
She clung to his brawn, like an injured fawn beseeches its
    mother's care,
And her gay perfume hung sweet in the room, like a garden of
    lilies fair.

That questioning brow looked up at him now, approval for
    better or worse.
"Yah! Let's have a drink!" said the pannicky gink— (O! Need I
    finish this verse?)
        *   *   *   *

The following day they continued to play and to caper a fancy
       stride:
For a man that's flush and fresh from the brush will spend it
       handsome and wide.
She made it a point that a boot-legging joint was the place of
       her heart's desire,
And the taxi could wait, at a high-rice rate, while they guzzled
       the liquid fire.
With a wandering gaze and his eyes ablaze, beseeching a
       quarrelling bout,
He would show his might in a drunken fight, or the bouncer
       would toss him out;
But a man that's tight is no good in a fight, so he found himself
       in the "klink."
His throat was wry and his guts were dry, for want of a damn
       good drink;
And the dame had blew, like her type so true, in cahoots with
       the "hair-decked lip."
He cursed and swore he'd drink no more—O God! for one little
       sip!

Now the "hair-decked lip" presented a slip that was signed for
       the ox-choking roll,
And Bill realized he was ostracized from cutting his fancy scroll.
for now he was broke as a twice told joke, so they paid him his
       fare to the brush.
he could pay them back with his hard-earned jack when he
       came back feeling flush.
So he gets on the boat, with a brown parched throat, sore ribs,
       and a big black eye.
He looked o'er the side—on the dock he spied a blond that was
       waving good-bye
To another guy, with tears in her eye; "Look me up next time
       you're in!"
Then she went her way with her feline sway, and looked for
       another to skin.

So "Pannicky Bill" of the brush and hill sat down and pondered
     his case:
O! What a fool and godblasted tool I've been for a feminine face!
I know I've been rolled, and the chokers cold will be heavy and
     kinky as hell;
And they'll clatter and ring, as they toss and swing and sound
     like a jangling bell.
The jaggers will rip till the blood I'll sip, with the sweat running
     down my cheek;
And the sing of the lines and the smell of the pines will whisper,
     "You sucker weak!"
But I'll do it again, like all other men who were born with the
     lust in the blood.
To sin and to dance, to love and romance, raise hell, while the
     raising is good!
So I guess I'll slave like a niggardly knave and save up another
     stake;
And I'll spend it free, with laughter and glee, and live—for
     living's sake!

        *   *   *   *

She stalks the street, her prey to meet, that she may dine and drink;
Through hennaed hair, to hide despair, she gives her beckoning wink:
With slinking bluff she totes her stuff on the blazing skid roads of sin
And she says good-byes with tears in her eyes and looks for another to
     skin.

THE WISE DONKEY PUNCHER

"I am the guy with the brains 'round here:
A wise, wise fellow—an engineer.
In the winter's cold I shiver and shake,
In the summer's heat I sweat and bake;
On topics great I know it all—
The Life of Christ or the Romans' Fall.
I know the cause of the strife today
And cures for such to me is play.
My brain is quick, my thinking clear:
I'm the 'donkey puncher'—the engineer.

"Ain't I the man who went to town?
Ain't I the guy who wrote it down?
To show Inspectors old and grey
How to set valves the proper way?
There on the wall all framed 'neath glass
My ticket proud of the donkey class.
A rigging buster from Hell and back
On the little old unit way up the track.
Gimme a boiler with lots of fog
And I'll show you guys just how to log.

"Now the hooker?—there is a funny guy.
Not in the class with such as I—
Won't come for advice like other birds,
But sits on a stump and mumbles words.
And the rigger! (the guy that tops the firs)
Clutters my box with 'belt and spurs';
And the loaders—the fools I always forget—
If they don't watch out, I'll get them yet.
The punk! The useless, lazy streak—
Ruins my ears with his whistle's squeak.

"On Sunday I love to put in the time,
I'm telling you boys it's a dirty crime
The way they've run this 'pot' to Hell.
What'll break next, it's hard to tell:
But I loosen this and tighten that
And crawl on the roof, like a prowling cat.
The blocks are worn, the gears have play
(But manage at least to put in the day).
I wash my pants and scrub my shirt
And steam-hose off the worst of the dirt.

"My haulback's so tight it cracks and sings,
Till I've burned and scorched my friction pins.
To keep my rigging high up in the air,
Back to the 'tail-holt'—way out there.
And still they kick (that rigging crew),
What in the Hell do they want me to do?
I'm sure those fools have choked a stump
And, sitting there in the shade on their rump,
Letting me reef and snort. They'll see—
I'll pull the top clean out of the tree.

"And so I do! The 'guys' go slack,
The 'soup' is walking up the track,
Slapping his thighs with his fancy hat
And cursing me, just for doing that:
The loaders crawl from beneath the cars
And stare in the air as if counting stars,
The crew walks in in a staggering group
The hooker hollers, 'You nincompoop!'
I pack my tools—to town I go
He's a haywire hooker, and I told him so!"

23

THE AMBITIOUS "PUNK"

Out in the brush with the rigging crew I sit me down on a chunk,
And I heed the call of the "hooker's" bawl, I'm an expert
    "whistle punk."
My coded "toot" to the engineer, that man we curse so free,
Will start the lines and the snapping chunks and the snorting in
    at the tree.

As the live main-line stretches skyward, a glistening ribbon of
    steel,
Its "bight" throwing saplings and windfalls with the speed of a
    flying teal.
I thrill as the choker-locked fir tree bows backward its fall
    through the air:
And the whitened shaft of the old pine snag, ground-rotted, will
    fall—God knows where.

In the Spring, when the sap is the highest and the bud is green
    on the fir,
The "hooter" hoots to his hen-mate, his "come-to-me-call," as it
    were.
It's the time of the slippery "buck-skin" and the turn "hangs up"
    on a stump
And the bark will fly like a bombshell, then it's great to be only
    the "punk."

And I watch the "tame-apes" a-wrestling, applying their fancy
    holt—
Maybe a "roll" or a "squaw-hitch," soon a "hiball," and off with a
    jolt;
Maybe a "come-back" or "tight line," so I toot my signal with
    ease,
To keep the puncher a-guessing, with a crew he can never just
    please.

O! how I hate to pull "strawline," when they're changing line in
    the brush,
Or a guy is hurt on the rigging and into the "tree" I must rush.
And I hate to punk on a "cold-deck" or to help on a "rig-up"
    crew—
It's then I can't sit on my "fanny," for there's jobs they will find
    me to do.

You know I'm inclined to be lazy, that's why I am "only the
    punk."
When the crew's in at night playing horseshoes, it's then I will
    lounge in my bunk.
And I hate to get up in the morning, I'm the last at the table to
    feed;
But I eat like a guy with a tapeworm—I'm a gutsy young logger
    indeed.

Some day I may hope to be smarter and to wrestle with rigging
    galore.
I might take a job on the chokers and I'll curse the "duplex" no
    more.
I might reach the peak of perfection and a rigger I'll turn out to
    be—
Or I might be only a bull cook; I'll wait, and I'll live, and I'll see.

THE VANISHING HOST

WE—were the monarchs of forest, to the west of the great
    Cascades,
South of the Queen Charlotte Islands, north of the Oregon
    glades,
Sinking our roots in the hillside and deep in the canyon's shades.

Hundreds of millions our numbers, kings of coniferous clan.
Ours were the valleys untrodden, unspoiled by the hand of man.
Ours were the slopes of the mountain, before the great cut
    began.

Douglas fir we were christened (as man must give us a name),
Deemed that our host were too mighty—fit home for his hunting
    and game.
Mighty machines he invented to log us and further his gain.
To log us—ah yes—but our saplings and progenitors of our race
Left broken and charred in the valley, dismal and dreary the
    place,
Glutted and ravished and smoking! Where once spread our
    sylvan grace.

Have mercy, O man! In your hurry pause yet ere onward you go
Slashing and cutting and burning the saplings of long, long ago—
A vanishing host of the forest, that centuries only can grow.

26

Douglas Fir and Western Red Cedar
Photo by Leonard Frank, courtesy Jewish Historical Society of BC

THE WOLF CREEK TRAIN WRECK

A headlight stabbed the darkness drear,
Shone on salal brush far and near,
Reflecting back the dew drops' shine,
And sheen from hemlock, fir and pine.
Drably the bluff that's cloaked in black
Echoed the side-rods' metered clack,
And billowed smoke in a trailing row
Flashed with the fire-box's ruddy glow.
The air now shook with rending "bark,"
Onward! She thundered through the dark.

Full forty cars of loaded logs
Followed behind like trailing dogs.
Each log-car wheel with "two-inch skid"
Rattled and shook its journal lid.
That hollow thump an drum-like sound
Shivered and shook the swampy ground;
And screech of flanges biting rail
Echoed their discord through the vale.

Sat in the cab with eagle eye,
The "hogger" watched the miles slip by.
Asked of the fireman if he'd seen
Whether the "board" was red or green?
Then checked by glance the gauges there,
Showing the pressure of the air;

With practiced hand reduction made,
To slow her speed on heavy grade;
Waited a moment—like to feel
If shoes had gripped on whirling wheel,
Then, glancing backward through the dark,
Saw for himself the brake-shoes' spark.

For thirty years old Frosty there
Had pulled a throttle. . . eased the air;
That sight ahead, twin rails of gleam,
Which distance makes more closer seem,
Brought to his mind his younger years:
His eagle eye now wet with tears—
    Thought of that face in youth he woo
    Thought of the day she said "I do!"
    Thought of a home where life was new.
Yearned for the years to backward roll,
In death he'd see that parted soul,
    That love of youth, so true!
But fate had rended them apart,
Leaving an ache within his heart,
    An ache which few men knew.

His moment's dream was quickly sped. . .
Reaching a cord above his head,
His whistle "rolled" o'er hill and ridge,
A warning shrill for Wolf Creek bridge:
Where stately Douglas fir tree bowed—
Lowered its crest of branches proud,
As wind-swept fury from the sky
Carried the drifting branches by.
Through lightning flashes, blinding light,
Onward she thundered through the night!

Way out ahead, old Frosty gazed,
While "buffer-beam" the rock cut grazed.
Through cut and fill with shining rail

Monotony marked the main line trail:
And curving now by mountain's wall,
Where trestle spans the Wolf Creek brawl,
A mighty fir tree of the hill
In wind-swept fury now lay still:
Had pierced the canyon's trestled span
And prostrate lay where waters ran.

The "hogger" spied the gaping break
Like darkened cloud on lucid lake!
But thought at first his sight had lied,
So closer scanned the engine's side:
Then realized that gaping gloom
Could end his run and seal his doom:—
"Big holed the air!" So chamber "Y"
From train line makes the air apply,
Flowing through ports like bullet freed,
Pressed on the brakes to check the speed.
Too late to halt momentum's weight,
The outcome rested now with fate!

A second's time seemed like a year.
As certain doom came closer near,
   And life seemed but a dream.
Hypnotic trance replaced his fear,
The sights of childhood reappear!—
   He eyed the swollen stream.
Too late to jump and wreckage clear—
A better end for an engineer
   To die by scalding steam!

They felt the bending timbers crack,
The drivers drop from off the track.
She lurched a second on the brink,
Then plunged like a plummet in the drink!
The steam pipes broken, they spewed their steam,

With hissing sound, like Hell's blaspheme;
That rose up skyward as a cloud,
While falling logs through trestle ploughed.
Soon all was silent but the brawl
And sighing wind through timbers tall.

*   *   *   *

A wrecking crew with ponderous hook,
When daylight came, the wreckage shook:
Lifting the cars with heavy gear,
For fireman looked and engineer.
They found old Frosty, cooked and dead,
Jammed up against the boiler head;
His broken watch from next his heart
Dropped on the deck and fell apart—
Revealing in that open case
The picture of a woman's face.

The fireman all besmeared with sand
Was clutching something in his hand,
His eyes were bulging out his head,
But bravely shouted out and said:
"Pick up the cab and free me loose,
This time she nearly cooked my goose!
This precious fluid I hold here
Is near and dear to the engineer.
I've cheated death and Hell's recoil,
But saved his precious can of oil."

THE BALLAD OF THE "SHANTY QUEEN"

'Twas down in the Grays Harbor country
    In nineteen thirty-three,
That Curly the rigger took him a wife
    To be queen of his camp shanty.
O! fair was her form as an angel
    And soft was the light in her eyes,
Her quizzical smile would a saint beguile.
    O! clever was she and wise.

At night, when the long day was over,
    And the big, red sun settled low,
They'd frolic like children together,
    Bathing in love's rosy glow.
Happy was Curly the rigger!
    Joyful contentment he knew;—
For love is a joy with assurance,
    That your mate is truer than true.

High up, in an old-growth fir tree,
    Was Curly the topper of firs,
He looked like a clinging Flicker
    Hung on by his belt and spurs.
When the top leaned dizzily over,
    And he swayed in circles around;
He thought of his wife in the shanty,
    So he climbed down the tree to the ground.

Maybe his darling was lonely,
    He'd surprise her, and early arrive.
O! lucky was he, and so happy!
    Forever their love would survive.
"What's this by his lonely shanty?
    A roadster with down-folded top!

Maybe a friend from the city,
   Stopped by, for a chat and a drop."

Now there's men that covet the woman
   That's wife to another man;
And such was Lewie the Traveller,
   With sneaking and covetous plan:
Not to steal and support her,
   But to lustfully fondle and sate;
To steal the right of a husband,
   To pilfer and chisel his mate!

And faith in the heart of the human
   Forever eternally springs:
But it sank in the heart of the rigger,
   Like a bell that's cracked, when it rings.
In the arms of Lewie the dandy,
   Was the wife of his bosom and soul.
She clung to that masterful lover,
   Like an actress when playing her role.

Ah, the curse of a man that's a satyr!
   His darling to purloin away.
A voice in his mind said "Revenge sir!
   Step in and the satyr you slay!"
But he shrank from the scene broken hearted,
   Then revenge within him arose—
"O God! in your heaven have mercy,
   He'll punish himself—as he goes!"

For the rigger, in true rigger's fashion,
   Had measured the height with his eye.
From two mighty trees by the roadside
   That height he had strung up a"guy"
Of"straw-line"a half inch in thickness,
   To bight on the windshield there;
As the satyr drove by in his hurry,
   'Twould shatter his visage so fair!

And so when the sun was a setting
   he went with a heavy breast.
Plodding his lonely pathway,
   That led to his broken love nest.
He was greeted with babbling chatter
   (For the guilty conscience must speak);
And never was she more alluring—
   Never more feline and sleek.

      *   *   *   *

Then a knock was heard on the panel;
   "Someone has just had a wreck!
A roadster is smashed and is twisted
   And the fellow's near broken his neck,
Caught by a piece of strawline!
   He's broken, and bruised, and marred.
By the cuts on the face of that fellow
   You can bet he will always be scarred!"

And such was the fate of the satyr,
   Lewie the wrecker of homes,
Who pilfered the love of the wedded,
   Now tortured and branded he roams;
And such is the law that is written:—
   "So shall the evil be scarred—
For they which are joined in wedlock. . .
   Let no man render apart."

THE ANSWER TO A HOOKER'S PRAYER

The wintry sun shed its slanting rays
That shone through the evergreen canopy's maze;
And the shadowed spell of the moody dell
Lay eerie and long on the swamp and fell.

The slumber of ages silence was broken
By cursing and laughter of loggers a-jokin',
And fallin' of pines, and snappin' of lines,
As "haulback" that's "siwashed" pulsingly whines.

Stood on a stump in his rain-test clothes,
Where yarding had left the chunks in rows,
And kicking a hunk of bark from the stump,
The hooker was cursing the crew and the punk.

"O! what a crew and a 'chicken crap' show!
Holy old, lightning old, Lord! but they're slow!
Their ways are styled like a four-year child,
And they don't know 'Shinola' from honey wild."

Just then came the holler of "Hi!"—and a toot,
And trees in the bight began to uproot;
With snapping of chunks and jangle and thumps,
As the turn crashed on over windfall and stumps.

but one forked stump, three "board holes" high,
Was sure to hang up e'er the turn went by . . .
no tight line chide that the hooker tried
Would flip the bight to the other side.

So to get some slack he reared her back,
And hollered and raved like a maniac;
With a curse and a cry,—threw his gloves on high,
Tossed back his head, and spoke to the sky:—

35

"Oh God! in your heaven come down—if you can!
Don't send me your son—it's a job for a man!
With marline-spike teeth and a breath of fire,
And whirl out the kinks from this choker wire."

Then a raven screamed!—and the whistle tooted,
The haulback slacked and the rigging scooted;
And caught in the bight of the chokers tight,
'Twas the last "hang-up" that hooker would fight.

Now strange as it seems it has often been spoke,
That many a truth is spoken in joke:
For God of our soul is watching us all,
'Tis said he can tell if a sparrow should fall.

And He must have heard—for the rigging was straight;
There wasn't a kink nor a "figure eight."
So when you defy the Highest of High,
Think of this tale—and the hook-tending guy.

THE KICK BACK OF FATE!

Billy and I were buddies of old and we'd worked in the mills for
    years;
He was "spotting" for me on the "edger" and keeping his eye on
    the "clears."
We were sneaking a smoke while the millwright was fixing a
    broken chain;
Full well, we knew that the "head-rig" would soon be a-whining
    again.

He confided in me like a brother, that day in the hot boiler
    room:
And told me his troubles of long long ago, of the day he was
    newly a groom:
He'd been framed on a verdict of murder, proven guilty beyond
    any hope;
But he'd skipped out of town on a freight train, escaped and had
    cheated the rope.

He went on to say how this fellow had framed him and ruined
    his life:
Had married the girl of his heart-strings and cheated him out of
    his wife.
Cruel fate! How she'd died broken-hearted, not knowing the
    truth of the case—
Of a trusting and God-fearing mother, and the agonized look in
    her face.

Last night while asleep in the bunkhouse those faces had flashed
    in a dream:
He had seen the dear form of his sweetheart and the smile of his
    mother serene;
They'd warned him of imminent danger, that detectives had
    followed his trail;

And soon they would all be together, up there . . . in the land
    past the veil.
So back to our work on the "edger," for the head-rig was
    screaming again;
Where the "carriage receded like thunder and the sawdust it
    pattered like rain.
The "cants" fell down on the "roll-case," with the boom of a
    Congo drum,
While the sawyer conversed with the "setter" in signs of the deaf
    and the dumb.

Did you ever stand in a sawmill and hear those unearthly sounds,
When the trimsaws barked and they jangled like the yapping of
    quarrelling hounds—
The dual-tone cry of the edger, distinctive of sawmilling lore,
While the timber-sizer continues with its "diapasonal" roar?

Well, a man in a mill only hears them when something is eating
    his heart,
And I heard them quite plainly that morning, as my helper was
    playing his part.
In his pitch-stained apron of belting, he seemed like a man in a
    trance;
I could see that his brain was a-thinking of the soul of that faded
    romance.

I must have been working subconscious, for I didn't see them
    come in;
but they strode down the floor with the foreman to the tune of
    that roar and din.
Their guns were drawn from their holsters—those uniformed
    men of the law—
Heading straight over to Billy, who stood in the line of my saw.

'Twas then that I saw it all happen—with the aim of a flying dart,
A "kick-back" flew out from the edger—got Billy just under the
    heart!

As he lay on his back in the sawdust, he whispered while
      gasping for air—
"Thanks, pal, you've done me a favor."Then his eyes took a
      fixed, glassy stare!
On his face was a smile of contentment, like he'd gazed on the
      land of the blest;
And I thought of his dream in the bunkhouse and his vision of
      loved ones at rest.
So you see, Cruel Fate can be kindly and sometimes will honour
      defend:
For Billy, he died as a martyr, not as a convict condemned.

THE VERSATILE CEDAR

Gloomy the dell and dismal the swamp, where roots of the
    Cedar tree thrive;
Theirs is the law of the forest, where only the strong shall
    survive,
Where might is right to reach the light, and might will the
    weaker deprive.

Bearded with moss as druids of old, sorrowful boughs of the
    gloom,
Theirs is a heritage moody, theirs is the evergreen plume:
Theirs is the wood of the Totem God, theirs is the board of the
    tomb.

Glistening spires greet the morning sun, where echoes the
    swamp-robin's cry—
Perch of the bald-headed eagle, surveying his prey from on high:
Theirs is the lair of the hibernant bear, denned up for the winter
    they lie.

Pole of the high-tension power line, staff for the Union Jack,
Wood of King Solomon's temple, yet shake of the pioneer's
    shack;
Prospector's friend to the bitter end, board of his frying-pan
    snack.

Odour that's death to the parasite moth, yet home to the wild
    honey bee.
Easy to fashion, slow to decay. . . O fortunate mortals are we
To have such a wood, so sound and so good, as the versatile
    Cedar tree.

Western Red Cedar
Photo by Leonard Frank, courtesy Jewish Historical Society of BC

PAUL BUNYAN WAS A PIKER

'Twas a "sky-line" show, with a yard of snow piled high on log
    and chunk,
And around a fire by the "whistle-wire" the crew were kidding
    the "Punk."
That jostling bunch were eating their lunch, and talking of
    screwball schemes,
When a "Choker-man" at once began to boast of big machines:
Of a twelve drum rig, with a boiler so big, the stack was as high
    as the spar!
With a playful shove, while drying his glove, the "Hooker" then
    started from par.

"Now I have a hunch, you Sunday-School bunch think donkeys
    are something with ears.
Punched, bored, nor drilled, you've never been thrilled by the
    rumble of ponderous gears.
Paul Bunyan's yarns of colossal barns, and tales of the big blue
    ox,
Are awfully tame and always the same; in fact, they're too
    orthodox.
So listen, you birds, to my truthful words of a tale of a big
    machine;
For I'm telling you that when I am through, you'll marvel at
    what I have seen.

"In a 'Redwood' show, a long time ago, way down in the
    'Sunshine' state;
Down where the crew have plenty to do and they log at a
    'hi-ball' rate.
They had a machine as long as a dream and as wide as a
    good-sized claim.
You talk of your drums! you home-guard bums should have seen
    the size of her 'main'!

42

A twelve-mile haul was nothing at all, her exhaust made clouds
    in the sky,
That fell down again in the form of rain, so a man could never
    keep dry.

"That ponderous rig was so God awful big! it's hard for a man to
    compare;
But to give you the gist, the fireman was missed, we looked and
    searched everywhere.
He was getting a drink, I'm inclined to think, and had fallen
    into the tank;
Though we grappled around, he couldn't be found—O! what had
    become of poor Hank?
So I looked in the glass, and there, alas, was our fog-promoting
    toiler—
Floating there loose, all cooked like a goose, in the glass on the
    side of the boiler.
Now perhaps you surmise the enormous size of the monster of
    big machines,
So you never should boast of 'pots' on the coast, like 'eleven by
    seventeens'!"

THE IMMORTAL FRASER

Mighty Fraser, ever wending through the valleys, through the
    canyons;
Through a delta to the ocean, near the peaks which are
    companions.
Born of ramparts in the Rockies, silver-capped with ancient
    snows,
Melting glaciers there are feeding the mighty Fraser as it
    grows.

'Neath the shadow of Mount Robson, lofty roof of Rocky
    Mountain,
Flowing northward, ever rolling, fed by cataract and fountain.
Turning southward, eddies swirling, in the country near Prince
    George;
Muddy waters, silt suspended, the mighty Fraser carves her
    gorge.

Onward! Onward! Ever wider, through the "Cariboo" of
    grazing,
Through the hills of naked beauty, ruddy sunsets glory blazing.
Dancing, rippling in the twilight, lonely river bathed in
    blood,
On to Lytton, where her waters meet the Thompson's turquoise
    flood.

Swollen now, that muddy turmoil, roaring forward to the ocean;
Through the canyon's barren splendor; on with thunderous,
    swirling motion.
Hell's Gate chasm! Have you seen it? Where the waters seethe
    and pound?
Where the salmon leap like fury? . . . Onward to their
    "spawning-ground."

On past Yale, through fertile valley; mighty stream of
     navigation.
Where the Siwash off to potlatch used canoe for transportation.
Birch and willow gently nestle, yellow grain, and fields of corn.
Through the delta's charted channel, ocean vessels safely borne.

*   *   *   *

Cities grow and nations prosper on the shores of mighty streams;
Humans die and are forgotten, life's so aimless—so it seems.
When the last of us shall perish, waning sunshine colder
     growing;
Mighty Fraser will meander, ever onward. . . slowly flowing.

THE SPIRIT OF THE FOREST

I'm the Spirit of the Forest; and I guard my silent host
That populate my mountain slopes and valleys to the Coast.
Like fabled gods of ancient Greece made home in mountain
      high,
My throne, the lofty Rockies, where they reach unto the sky;
The thunder clap my angered voice; the sighing trees my lyre,
The sinful deeds of Satan are to me the forest fire.

I'm queen of the countless canyons, king of a million peaks;
Nymph of my timbered valleys green and lord of my swollen
      creeks;
Ruler of flowing glaciers, God of Eternal Snows;
Mother of giant conifers and every shrub that grows;

46

Spawn of the swamp-loving Cedar, seed of the long-needled
       pine;
Crown of the stately Douglas Fir, but the Human is not mine.

Oh puny man with earth-bound greed dare trespass in my lair;
Strings up his spider web of steel, to log my valleys fair.
Doth take the best and leave the rest, lays waste my slumbering
       dell;
So the forest fires of Satan can play infernal Hell:
To char my infant saplings, the children of my womb.
Leaves naught but stark desolation, black snags to mark their
       tomb.

Ere man became so contriving, my forests afforded him home;
Lived in the heart of my splendors, where turbulent cataracts
       foam:
Nurtured him like as my offspring, fed him from out of my breast;
Took unto me his fleeting soul, his mortal bones laid at rest.
Now he's created his cities, is lord of his own domain;
When he destroys his existence, my forests will thrive there
       again.

THE TRADE TEST OF SAINT PETER

A scientist man was weary of life on this earthly shore,
So he died and went up to heaven, where 'tis said life lasts
  evermore.
At the gate he was met by Saint Peter, who was hoary and
  grizzled with age.
The Doomsday Book lay opened and turned to a special page.
He glanced at the man of science, who was standing there in the
  nude.
Said Saint Peter, "Where is your toga? Aren't you the scientist
  'dude'—
The man of theorem and figures? Why haven't you figured a way
To get your 'junk' past the reaper? Let's hear what you have to
  say!"

Said the man of slide-rule and figures: "Don't you know I'm a
  clever gent?
Down there I've worked and I've sweated, but never had time to
  invent
A gadget in seventh dimension, to do just the simple 'jerk'
Of taking my worldly possessions to Heaven to finish my work."
"To Heaven!"said bearded Saint Peter. "What makes you think
  you will go
To that land of celestial beauty, and not down to Hades below?"
"Oh no!"said the spirit of science. "You won't put me in that
  hole!
I'd be useful to you up in Heaven, on formula good for the soul."

"On Earth,"said the spirit of theory, "I'll tell just what we
  achieve:
We're making our rubber synthetic, so good that it's hard to
  believe.
We've a chap who is splitting the atom with a special wave of
  'X-Ray':

48

And another has made a reflector to examine the Milky Way.
One of us made television, another perfected a light
That burns with a wire incandescent, like rays of the Sun in the
    night.
A genius fashioned an auto and another invented the 'tank,'
The 'aero-plane' was developed—down there in the land of the
    'Yank.'"

He went on to say to Saint Peter: "We scientist men have our
    fun.
There's nothing we like to do better than to think up a new type
    of gun,
One that shoots faster and faster, and deals out a horrible death;
And we love to scheme and to ponder on a gas that will stifle
    the breath."
"By Jove,"said Saint Peter, "you're clever! We might use a fellow
    like you.
If not, I am sure Mr. Satan will have jobs you are able to do.
So I want you to do something simple; if you cannot, poor
    fellow, alas!
I'll send you down there into Hades. So make me just one
    BLADE OF GRASS."

THE END OF DILLINGER'S TRAIL

A siren screamed its piercing howl from the top of the jail house
  tower,
And swinging plays of the search-light rays lit up each nook and
  bower;
A convict crawled along in a ditch and fooled them by his ruse,
The *Morning Herald* extra screamed the latest jail break news:—

"A cop was killed and a trusty drilled, as Dillinger broke on the
  loose,
His mind was crazed, his reason dazed by fear of a knotted noose,
He'd sat and moped like a guy that's doped and stared at the
  one-way door;
He'd wanted to cry and hated to die, he'd cursed and prayed and
  swore."

"The prison priest his soul had greased to slip through heaven's
  gate.
Though black as coal, his whitewashed soul a flute and harp
  should rate:
But men of crime, they bide their time and know no rule nor
  law,
Wild chances take to make their break, with nerves all ragged
  and raw.
"That man of sin had smuggled in a hacksaw (just the blade),
He'd sawed the bars beneath the stars, a groove was slowly made.
At last with knife, a fight for life!—He'd grabbed the jailer's gun!

The bars were spread—a 'trusty' dead, the gauntlet apparently
    run."

*   *   *   *

Now escape he made as bloodhounds bayed, and sniffed the
    sloppy mire,
But gangster John relied upon the prison "grapevine wire,"
When in a "jam" and on the "lam" to head for "Sloppy Joe's,"
And this he did, and so he hid, with shelter, food and clothes.

It wasn't long before his throng of thieves and racketeers
Were robbing banks and shooting Yanks, like gangster
    bombardiers:
But men so rough get mighty tough and reckless in their ways—
Don't comprehend that in the end—such crime, it never pays!

He kept a "moll," a painted doll, all dressed in silk and frills,
And talked too light with boasting might of escapade and kills:
Made that mistake, which most men make, put trust in woman's
    breast,
He might have known her heart of stone could never stand the
    test.

No tooth nor nail of county jail could keep him in the "can,"
Though catch they did he "blew the lid," assisted by his clan;
And "bopped" the cop who tried to stop, his gang which set him
    free;
With murderous threat, he slipped the net and left the cops at
    "sea."

But the eagle eye of the F.B.I., who always spot their man,
Those "Hoover dicks," of sleuthing tricks, had figured out a plan;
They'd bait the hook, which Adam took, to plunge the world in
    sin.
They'd pay the dame of gangster's fame his confidence to win.
So in due time that man of crime had set his mind to scan
A picture good from Hollywood, about a gangster man.

'Twas called "Big House," with "Mickey Mouse" as an extra
    feature showing;
And, strange but true, there were but few racketeers could stop
    from going.

So dressed in red from foot to head, she steered him to the show.
With interest keen, he watched the screen, forgot his cares and
    woe;
Suspecting not their crafty plot, their ruse in female form,
He rose to go from out the show—the lull before the storm!

And what a storm in battle form to greet him in the street!
She stepped aside to save her hide, for "Gangster John" was beat!
Quick as a flash he made a dash for freedom down a lane,
But cops (his dread) with a bead on his head, were plugging lead
    in his brain!

His dying thoughts were childhood days, a mother worn with
    care—
Telling her boy of Heaven's joy, he could see her rocking there:
But he'd placed his trust in passion's lust, and heeded the Devil's
    say!
And now he knew his days were through—that crime, it doesn't
    pay!

Such was the end of Dillinger's trail, the death of the gangster of
    fame;
Who beat the rope and Heaven's hope, and played a losing
    game.
His dying word was all we heard: "Come closer while I say—
'Never trust a woman!' and 'Crime, it doesn't pay!'"

THE DYING LOGGER'S LAMENT

Oh! Were I back on a Union boat, heading home for the jungle
    once more,
In a logging camp by a railroad track, where the snorting "locies"
    roar.
Where the flunkie rings the "second bell," and I hear the crunch
    of caulked feet,
Like rampant steers go through a gate, I head for my own certain
    seat.

I gorge myself till I nearly bust, yet I don't sit there very long'
Though while I do, I make her pay, my appetite's awfully strong.
I top her off with hotcakes ten, fried eggs and "dunked" "hard
    tack,"
And pick my teeth as I leave the place, soon I'm heading
    out—up the track.

And the speeder smells like Hastings Street, with the fumes
    from the engine there.
It jogs my mind of how I was rolled in town on a drunken tear!
She'd seen me off at the Union Dock, then looked for another to
    skin,
And said to be sure to look her up when I blew back to town
    again.

I would work, and slave, and sweat, and curse, and wrestle with
    rigging galore;
Or swing an axe, or pull the tongs, till my back's near broken
    and sore.
It's a damned hard life, but I've liked it all, and I've earned it the
    damned hard way,
And I've spent it free on Cordova Street, when I went into town
    to play.

I've hired to the Queen Charlotte Islands, where the Spruce and
    the Hemlock grows,
And I've shivered and shook on the rigging, in water-soaked
    mackinaw clothes.
I lay and I suffered in silence, in hospital, up at Rock Bay;
And poker I've played by the thousand hours, I've squandered
    my substance away.

Oh the dizzy dames that I've toted around, on the blazing
    skid-roads of sin!
And the dollars I've squandered and wasted, on whisky,
    demerarra and gin.
Those lewd and sinister faces, that taunted me back into town!
The urge to break the Commandment, by Moses so well written
    down.

In a cheap, lousy flop house I'm dying; my worldly possessions
    are few;
The landlord will sell them for room rent, to a spectacled Main
    Street Jew.
There's no one who cares to be sorry, and no one to shed any
    tears;
For I've burned my bridges behind me, and I've logged and
    squandered my years.

Now it looks like my days are ended and it seems that my life has
    been cursed,
Forlorn, forsaken and friendless, and weary of life at its worst.
I'll be glad to cash in when it's over and I'm carried away from
    this dump;
Don't fool around with a tombstone, boys—just bury me back of
    a stump.

L'ENVOI

Free souls are we who toil in Western brush,
True sons of Nature's solitude and hush;
 And we live a manly life,
 Where the elements run rife:
Removed afar from city's roaring rush.

I've tried your city's man-made noise and blare,
'Neath Neon's luminescence, blaze and glare;
 And I've longed for smell of pines,
 Snapping chunks and sing of lines,
And a lung full of that fragrant mountain air.

Where sunset's blazing glories paint the sky;
And snow capped mountains rear their peaks on high.
 In a Western wonderland,
 In the palm of Nature's hand
Is the heritage which Loggers occupy.

No weakling son of comfort shall be ours,
No purse-proud fledgling born of pomp and powers;
 For we live by brawn and might,
 Not by background and birthright;
But by brotherhood of man—where timber towers.

The artist's gift of painting is not mine,
I'd rather write and Loggers' ways define;
 And I've tried to tell the truth,
 (Pure, unvarnished, though uncouth)
Of sons of Nature in a Western clime.

STEEL TOWER
SKIDDER SHOW

HIGH-LEAD
SHOW

SKY-LIN

HAY-WI

SKY LINE

SLACK PULLING LINE

SKIDDER LINE

CHOKER LINE

RECEDING LINE

B L P

Timber

SLACK SKY LINE

MAIN LINE

CHOKER LINE

HAUL BACK LINE

AY

Photo by Leonard Frank, courtesy Jewish Historical Society of BC

BOOK II:

RHYMES
OF A
LUMBERJACK

I lay no claim to poet's fame,
    Where great immortals wallow;
Celestial fire does not inspire
    My printed page to follow.
My songs are songs for the outdoor throngs,
    In the Great Wide Open Spaces,
Where the mountains soar and the axes ring;
Where the rivers roar at the call of spring,
    When the log-jammed freshet races.

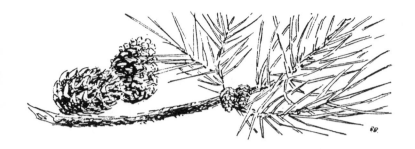

LIFE IN THE WESTERN WOODS

Journey west across the prairie, cross the Rocky Mountain
    ranges;
Gaze in wonder as you pass them—monuments of time-wrought
    changes.
Soon you'll reach the Western Forest, see the stately fir tree
    swaying;
See the drooping, moody cedar shade the brook where trout are
    playing.
        Lordly land away out yonder
           How you beckon—call me back.
        Oh! to wander, just to wander
           Through your dells—a lumberjack.

There to hear a donkey's whistle; feel the yarding donkey shiver;
See the main-line stretching skyward; watch the soft ground
    heave and quiver;
See the mighty logs come walking—crash through windfalls as
    they hurry;
Hear them thud beneath the spar-tree; watch the chaser jump
    and scurry.
        Now the duplex roars defiance,
           Loaders toss their tongs afar;
        Watch them juggle, watch their science,
           Loading logs upon the car.

See the steel-nerved rigger climbing mighty spruce with axe to
    top them;
Drooping limbs from view may hide him—swings his saw with
    ease to crop them;
Hear his axe ring through the valley—now, the top comes
    swishing downward!
See—he sits upon its zenith—rolls a smoke while gazing
    groundward.
    Echoes swell from timber falling,
        Whistles echo through the dells;
    Blended with the hooker's bawling,
        Chokers ring like jangling bells.

See the blood-red Forest Demon, fringed with tongues of blazing
    fury,
Glut the slashings, burn the saplings—see the deer before him
    hurry:
Crown fires sweep the lofty tree tops, leave behind stark
    desolation.
Worthy woodsmen fight this demon; spare the woods such
    devastation...
    Now the glutted valley smoulders,
        Smell the smoke that drifts around:
    Hillside strewn with crumbling boulders—
        Seed is parched from out the ground.

Come with me unto this woodland—watch the fawn creep low
    to cover;
Watch the dawn upon the hilltop greet the sun as a bride her
    love.
Fare thee well, O great metropolis, cruel and artificial city,
Here's one lumberjack who's leaving your maddened mobs,
    devoid of pity.
    Take me back, O fragrant forest,
        'Neath your pine trees let me dream;
    Let me join that woodland chorus
        Out where Nature reigns supreme.

PAUL BUNYAN'S ARCHIVES

There are tall tales told of a legend old, from the West Coast clear to
  Maine,
Of the Blue Ox Babe, Paul Bunyan's aid, that would tantalize your
  brain;
There are yarns galore of logging lore that are strange and far-fetched,
  too.
But for pastime's fun this takes the bun, 'cuz it proves those tales are
  true.

On a timber cruise, where you don't get news (but you
  sometimes hear a joke),
We had tramped all day, and at night we lay inhaling the camp
  fire's smoke.
'Neath a big windfall, in the timbers tall, we sat there toasting
  our toes,
In a circle of light, in a sea of night, where the tree trunk
  columns arose,
And it seemed you could hear, now far, now hear, the brawl
  from a canyon's brink,
Or a rubbing tree creaked parody to every thought we'd think.
The wolf-pack's cry, from the bluffs nearby, re-echoed its
  mournful wail,
As Hi-Ball Bill began to spill this tall Paul Bunyan tale.

"Now this mythical Paul," said old Hi-Ball, "was the acme of
  logging perfection,
For he and his ox piled the mighty rocks of the great Coast
  Range projection.
That ox's bellow was deep and mellow, yet as loud as a thousand
  bassoons,
And its eyes glowed bright in the dead of the night, like two
  luminescent blue moons.

So great was its size that between those eyes was a forty-nine
    axe-handle span;
And the giant Paul, thought stupendously tall, was a kind and
    benevolent man.
The Puget Sound he dug out of the ground was a place for Babe
    to wallow,
And Babe's appetite when feeling right—twelve tons of hay he'd
    swallow.
Oh it sounds like a crack from a maniac, whose reasoning
    powers have been twisted;
But the proof I found, deep down in the ground, that the Big
    Blue Ox existed.

"It was back in the years when we logged with steers and
    considered that donkeys were freaks;
In the virgin brush, where the white streams rush from the
    snow-clad Cascade peaks.
Now you'll open your eyes when I tell you the size of some of
    those forested giants,
For the size of those trees would an Einstein tease and baffle the
    annals of science.
So huge they were (both cedar and fir) that days were spent in
    their falling,
And the ground would shake with an evil quake, for their
    thunderous crash was appalling;
but the prize of them all that we started to fall had the growth of
    profusion attained,
And I knew in a trice without eyeing it twice—this monster was
    Bunyan ordained.

"Three days we chopped, and chopped, and chopped, three days
    from dawn 'til dark!
Three nights we chopped and never stopped; but didn't get
    down through the bark.
Now there was a tree, believe you me!—what made it so big was
    a mystery.

When the peaks were frozen over, and Paul
was thirsty, Babe would breathe on the glaciers.

So we stopped for a talk, and we took a walk, while we pondered
over its history;
And we compassed its flank, like a river bank—in and out of
each root-flanked canyon,
'Til we watched the sun when the day was done hand the night
to its fairer companion.
The soft, pale light from that moon at night loomed its trunk to
the heavens careening,
And I pinched my flesh to remind me afresh that surely I
couldn't be dreaming.

"We trekked in and out and around about the columns that 'rose
from its base;
'Til we seemed to sense, with a feeling tense, that we trod in a
hallowed place;
That our lives we'd dreamed. . . until now it seems we were
insects, merely creeping. . .
Then I heard a shout, and I turned about, and I knew that I
hadn't been sleeping:
'Twas another crew—and the great ships flew from the trunk of
that very same tree
From whence we had tried, on the opposite side, to unravel its
mys-ter-y;
But it wasn't no use. . . they'd run out of snoose, and the tree was
too God-awful big:
So they joined our force as their only course, and the bunch of
us started to dig.

"Now we didn't say quit 'til we'd burrowed a pit at its base, in
search of a clue—
In hopes we'd discover and maybe uncover the proof that my
hunch had been true.
Then, an oxen's yoke, all splintered and broke, was unearthed
from the depths down there,
And *Babe* was inscribed on its petrified side—and I noticed a
monstrous blue hair!

There were harness rings—big, ponderous things, and a diary
  carved in the rocks
That told us the story, the power and the glory of Paul and his
  Big Blue Ox.
So we buried them there with reverent care to preserve them
  from civilization,
And to finish my yarn—'twas the site of Babe's barn, and the
  acme of fertilization!"

There are tall tales told of a legend old, from the West Coast clear to
  Maine,
Of the Blue Ox Babe, Paul Bunyan's aid, that would tantalize your
  brain;
There are yarns galore of logging lore that are strange and far-fetched,
  too.
But for pastime's fun Bill took the bun when he proved those tales are
  true.

GOOD BYE, OLD TIMER

There she rusts among the fireweed;
  Silent now, this puffing toiler.
Alders grow between her axles—
  Twine their branches 'round her boiler.
Robbed and gone—her whistle's looted;
  Dulled and tarnished is her bell.
Could she speak, this locomotive,
  Oh, the stories she might tell!

Stories, strange, of booming savor;
  Tales of railroad men—departed;
Boomer hoggers and their firemen,
  How they groomed her, ere she started;
How they set their old-time hand brakes—
  Crushed their limbs with link-and-pin;
Heavy grades, and no dispatching—
  How she snorted—wheeled them in.

Time wings on to new horizons;
  Leaves behind its many changes
Monuments of bygone eras—
  Thus its landmarks Time arranges.
Logging trucks now scour the valley,
  Time hath given them their lease.
You and I are now discarded—
  Rust, Old Timer—rust in peace.

THE TAME APES

Tame apes of the jungles they call us,
  He-men of the forest are we;
Who spend our money on poker and booze,
And don't give a damn if we win or lose,
And a carefree life in the forest we choose,
  On the slopes, by the Western Sea.

We live a tough life when we're working,
  We play just as rough in the town;
We're suckers for women who wear high heels,
With well-moulded bodies and looser ideals,
That trip down the street, dolled up in their seals—
  Just waiting for us to come down.

We paint the town red when we're spending,
  It's drinks on the house by the crock.
Then our friends are many, and women smile.
It's "What is your hurry? Please tarry a while."
But then she's all spent—we walk the last mile
  Down to the Union dock.

Then it's "Give you an upper? The hell you say!
  You bums can sleep on the floor!"
The world seems cold, and people will shun,
But a tame-ape brother won't see you outdone—
He's still got a crock!. . . the son-of-a-gun!
  So you step in his stateroom door.

"Say!. . . Who's pushin' camp up at Kelley's?
  They tell me they're runnin' full slam"
Now the air is blue with cigarette smoke—
Someone is trying to tell you a joke;
You kinda forget you're goin' back broke
  To the jungles: but who gives a damn?

"We paint the town red when we're spending"

So back to the jungles you're headin' once more—
   To the brush where the tame-apes roam;
To a little old camp, by a railroad track,
Where the blue smoke curls from the bull cook's shack,
And the smell of a bunkhouse welcomes you back.
   By Gawd! but you soon feel at home.

And before dawn breaks in the morning,
   From his bunk will the tame-ape roll.
While still it is dark, he heads for the brush;
When the push-ape hollers, he'll scramble and rush—
Get down on his knees, in the cold, camp slush,
   And scratch for his choker-hole.

Soon the hooker will holler for straw-line:
   Then the apes in the brush go mad.
One runs with the end up a side-hill, sheer;
When he hollers out "Line!" you'll get in the clear,
And bound over logs and chunks like a deer;
   If you're slow . . . well, it's just too bad.

Then you think of the stake that you squandered,
   And the plans that you conjured before;
So you make them again, in the very same way—
You'll head into town with your hard-earned pay . . .
But you know in your heart you'll be king for a day,
   Then come back to the woods once more.

But life to a woodsman is freedom,
   Not measured in dollars sublime;
but to come and to go and quit when he please,
Not beg for a job on his bended knees,
Nor toadie to tycoons, with rich properties,
   Who would see him in Hell—for a dime.

A LOGGER'S TEN COMMANDMENTS

These are the Sacred Commandments, the rules by which loggers
  abide;
Laws of a life in the forest — as true as the laws of the tide.
Hearken and profit, then, stranger; hear ye the laws I confide:

Never sit down at the table to eat where another should sit.
This is the cause for a battle, that man is just li'ble to quit.

Wander not into the cookhouse before the guthammer has rung;
Cooks, as a rule, swing a cleaver — they're bitter and flippant of
  tongue.

Grab as the food is passed by you; for service don't bother your
  mate.
Speed is the essence of manners — your saucer should rest on
  your plate.

Praise nothing that's new 'til it's proven, but wait for the *super* to
  praise;
Supers alone have the brain-power to merit a thing by its ways.

Of a man, you should speak as you find him, though others may
  brand him a cur;
It may be his good reputation has been marred by a slanderous
  slur.

Money when saved is a worry, so never your pleasure deprive;
Live for today and be happy, tomorrow may never arrive.

Be lavish when spending your money, as a cheapskate never be
    caught;
There's nothing so low as the logger who says he is broke—when
    he's not.

Lines are your friends if you know 'em, but deadly as bullets in
    flight;
Give 'em respect and your distance, and never stand there in the
    bight.

Timber-r, when *falling*, means danger; stand well up above in the
    clear.
Sharp lookout will cheat undertakers, who gloat on a widow's
    sad tear.

Care you should have in the summer—for fire in a forest is crime.
Fire can destroy in a minute the growth of a century's time.

Now these are the Sacred Commandments, the rules by which loggers
    abide;
Laws of a life in the forest—as true as the laws of the tide.
Break them and suffer, then, stranger—they're ancient, and proven,
    and tried.

THE RHYME OF THE BIG SWEDE LOGGER

By da yumpin'yiminy yesus,
　　Aye yust kum back fr'm town,
Ay've seen da voman's fayces
　　In da spots off ill renown;
Ay've hire da fastes'taxies—
　　Had da best in effry house,
Got drunk on beer an'viskey—
　　Yust ass cray-see ass a louse;
An' aye tol' da fancey vomans
　　How ve log out in da voods—
How us Swenska super-humans,
　　Us alone produce da goods.
An' aye tol' da pretty maiden
　　How ve log in vinter's snow,
Wen aye kum out here from Swaden
　　Yust fifteen years ago.

An' wen firs' Aye kum dis countree
　　From ma native Swenska land,
Da language here seem funny
　　An' wass hard to understan':
For dey had a drink at mealtime,
　　An' dey call it *koffeeplease*,
But it taste yust like da coffee
　　Back in Sweden, cross da seas.

74

An' *winniger-yug* aye learn to say.
    Wen fifteen years had gone
Dey changed da name, an' so today—
    Dey call it *demi-yon*.
Dey might fool me wi' dere talkin'—
    Say ayme domb, an' green, an' shy:
But a Swede iss born to loggin'
    Like an eagle's born to fly.

W'en first aye hit da yungle,
    To me da fooreman said:
You'll neffer make a bungle,
    Iff you'll only youse yer head.
Go out an' wrestle schokers,
    An' be careful w'ere ya yump;
But da riggin' crew were yokers,
    An' so aye schoked a stump:
Aye used ma head to stop da huke
    Dat floated tru' da air—
An' here's da boomp—yust take a look,
    Protrudin' tru' ma hair.
Ay'me wiser now, since aye have learned
    Ma head's to hold my hat,
An' aye get along vit' all concerned
    W'en aye youse it yust fer dat.

At first aye tank dis countree
    Wuz yust scrum an' froth an' foam,
An' aye miss da Swenska yentry,
    An' da customs back at home.
Here ya doff yer hat to no one,
    Fer ya find yer yust ass good
As da banker, or da showman,
    Or da splitter of da wood.
Here are land vere winding inlets,
    Vit da mountain walls are shored!

75

Reflecting golden sunsets—
  Like ma native Swenska fjord.
Ma adopted land of freedom,
  From da Rio Grande to Nome,
Fer ay've said good bye to Swaden,
  An' aye tank aye don't go home.

THE LEGEND OF THE SPRUCE

Where the sun sinks low in scarlet
Rise the Islands of Queen Charlotte;
    Western rim of the Forest Empire 'cross the seas.
Land of drizzling rain and showers;
Land where the Godly Spruce tree towers;
    Land where Nature's Spirit lives in mighty trees.

There the Hemlock's crown arises,
Through the moody gloom it rises,
    Interlacing with the limbs of Sitka Spruce:
But the spruce becomes the master,
Pushing upward, growing faster,
    'Till its mammoth trunk is the forest's prize produce.

Legend says: In times historic
Lived the Goddess Sitka Doric
    And a prophet of the forest side by side;
And this prophet saw a vision,
That in fleeting Tim's transition
    Men would come to burn and waste their forest wide.

So they sought these northern island,
Changed the climate—raised the highland;
    Changed to Spruce and Hemlock trees forevermore,
So that Man with his destruction,

Greed for power and high production,
   Would find those trees too mighty on their shore.

Here, beside the broad Pacific,
On these isles they'd be prolific,
   Here, their Godly race of timber now abide.
And to prove the Gods begot them,
Nature's love has ne'er forgot them —
   Sitka Spruce and Western Hemlock — side by side.

THE DEATH OF ROUGH HOUSE PETE

At the top of a darksome stairway, on a two-bit flophouse cot,
Old Rough House Pete lay down his weary head;
For his rough house days were over, and his last hangup was fought.
Ere he closed his bloodshot eyes, old Rough House said:

"In the days of bull-team logging, when they hauled logs on the
    skid,
    And they cut the stumps 'way up above the swell;
It was then I hit the jungles—I was only just a kid,
    But the roughest, toughest kid this side of Hell.
I could lick a cougar cat, if a man should drop the hat,
    And I'd kick my way from jail with flying feet:
California to Alaska—I was famous for just that,
    And so, far and wide they hailed me, 'Rough House Pete.'

"When the bull teams all were finished and the ground-lead
    donkey came,
    And the line-horse days had gone beyond recall!
I had hired to do the hookin'—up at Simoon Sound of fame,
    But the camp and cook were haywire—grub and all.
On the table-top jumped I, and made the dishes fly,
    You can bet my old caulk-shoes weren't very slow.
Then the *Cassiar* I boarded, and I bade that camp good-bye,
    And they stowed me with the cattle down below.

"Oh, those trips aboard that steamboat, up and down this rugged
    coast;
    How the skipper, mate and deck-hands feared my tread.
All the doors were kicked to splinters—each railing, stair and
    post;
    When I'd step aboard each time, the skipper said:
Man the pumps and test the hose—all the first-class quarters
    close;

79

For Rough House Pete has stepped aboard my ship.
I would rather face a blizzard when a North-East howler blows,
  Than to have that man aboard for just one trip!'

"Came the days of high-lead logging and the fast machines of
    steam.
  You can bet old Rough House Pete was with the first
To be foreman of an outfit, way out near Aberdeen;
  But, I met a girl, and then my life seemed cursed.
O, that throbbing urge of Nature—how a man can be a fool—
  Can be weak as rotten straw-line in her grip;
For the lion may be monarch, but the lioness more cruel,
  With her silken claws, defiles his championship.

"O, I know I went soft-hearted and I tried my ways to mend,
  And we lived like honest people on the square.
But a match not sealed in Heaven is most surely doomed to end,
  And I came home late one night—she wasn't there!
So I packed my bags; Hell bent to Seattle town I went,
  When I found she'd left with Johnnie-on-the-Spot.
By the Gods! I swore, I'll kill him!'—Many days and nights I spent
  In Seattle's tenderloin, but found them not.

"But the gears of Time roll surely, 'til at last all cogs must mesh,
  And Coincidence seems but the hand of Fate;
For in Barney's bar one evening stood that traitor in the flesh:
  At the sight of him, my blood boiled hot with hate.
Not with guns we fought that meet, but with fists and caulk-shod
    feet;
  With the joint near wrecked, at last I had him down.
Then they drank a toast on Barney: 'To the victor, Rough
    House Pete.'
  Then I took the *Cassiar* and sailed from town.

"Oh those years of fights and boozing, and of all-night poker
    games,
  How I've worked and toiled in sunshine, rain and sleet.

80

Rough House Pete kicking hell out of the dishes!

How I've blown my toil-earned dollars on a lot of skidroad
  dames,
And I'm dying now with caulk shoes on my feet.
Yet, all might have been serene, if that dame from Aberdeen
  Had led me down the straight and narrow way:
All my toil and tribulation for my family might have been;
  But I'm dying now—and don't know how to pray.

". . . Queer, how the lights grow dimmer. . . my feet feel cold and
  numb,
  And before my eyes I see my wasted years. . .
I can hear a donkey's whistle. . . Slack her down! Hey, roll that
  drum!. . .
  Wake up there, punk!. . . or else clean out those ears.
. . . I'll be late tonight, my darling; for the crew's out fighting
  fire. . .
  Yes, I'll kill the man who stole my love away. . .
Now my eyes are closing heavy—just to sleep is my desire. . .
  Oh God. . . I've tried, but I don't know how to pray. . ."

It was thus this roughneck woodsman told his tale of grief and woe,
  Ere his voice trailed off within that dingy room.
There was none to stand there weeping on the day we laid him low,
  And no shaft of marble raised to mark his tomb.
Yet, it's strange how Mother Nature, with her all-consuming scheme,
  To her breast will always claim the dust she gave.
For today, a sapling fir tree reaches up its branches green,
  While it sinks its roots deep down in Oleson's grave.

SEATTLE RED

Now, this is the tale of Seattle Red,
Who had auburn hair on the top of his head.
He could curse and swear, and rave and tear;
Laugh to beat Hell; yet crab like a bear.

He'd worked on the coast north of Mexico,
From the Sunshine State to Alaska's snow;
And he roamed around and covered the ground,
For he toiled in the woods as a timber-hound.

You could hear him holler for twenty miles —
Echoing long, in the timbered wilds.
We could always tell his high-pitched yell,
For it sounded much like a noise out of Hell.

But women!... Bah! They were nertz to him
(Unless they were blond and trim of limb),
For I heard him say on Yesler Way
He picked up a dame by the name of Fay.

Said Red to the dame, "Now don't you think
That you and me should have a drink?"
She nodded her head, in approval said,
"A drink it shall be, with Seattle Red."

83

Oh, what a woman of cultured poise
Now clung to that muscle-bound man of noise;
In a sequined gown, she showed him the town,
From the gyppo flops to the spots of renown.

But at least Red's dough was "gone-with-the-wind,"
Like virtue's gone, when a maiden has sinned,
And the fancy dame, with the fancy name,
Left with the grace and ease . . . that she came.

So now he was flat as a stale hot-cake,
Squandered and gone was his hard-earned stake:
No dough for a bed, and sore was his head:
Ah! such was the plight of Seattle Red.

Then he made this vow: "By the Gods above,
Deliver my soul from the lures of love.
It's plain to see, love's not for me—
I'm off women for life, by the holy gee!

"I'll have my fun out of automobiles,
With sneak-away tops and fancy wire wheels:
Double ignition, with air-condition,
And gadgets galore, will be my ambition."

So, back to the woods, where the stately trees
Bask in the sun or sway in the breeze,
Where the echoes die in the mountains high,
As the tame-apes bellow and holler "Hi! Hi!"

By the sweat of his brow Red saved up his pay,
And stayed in camp for many a day.
At last, with a grin, he pulled the pin,
And went into town—his fun to begin.

Oh! what a demon of supercharged power...
(Streamlined, indeed, to the trend of the hour)
Was his pride and joy to tinker and toy,
And burn up the county roads—yeah, boy!

*   *   *   *

But the vows of men and their sage advice
Soon dribble and drip—like a cake of ice;
For a red little head in a trundle bed
Is the new found joy of Seattle Red.

IN THE WIND OF HUMAN SCORN

This hollow smile beneath my rouge is but a fiendish lie
To hide the shame upon my soul. . . my burden till I die.
An outcast wreck from the homes of men, I drift upon Life's
stream,
And I make men pay in my sordid way for a shattered girlhood
dream.

When, but a girl of seventeen, I cherished Virtue's joy,
And knew not then the ways of men, but acted shy and coy,
I placed my trust in the human heart. . . believed in love's sweet
plan;
But the storms of Fate changed love to hate, in a world that's
ruled for man.

A wedding ring, falsely betrothed, a lamb to slaughter led:
For love's first kiss unlocked my heart, brought shame upon my
head.
'Twas just a step from Virtue's path, and then—too late to learn
That once you're in this game of sin. . . no woman shall return.

And man's brute strength has woman ruled since first the light
of day,
And man has made me what I am—so duly man must pay.
My soul is dead; my body lives; my heart is granite, cold;
The vultures feed with lustful greed—but first I take their gold!

I take their gold. . . the lust-lorn brutes, both young and old the
    same;
And he who hires my bartered love but shares with me my
    shame.
So has it been since Time began—each man must have his fling,
Should woman yield. . . her fate is sealed as a lewd and callous
    thing.

My secret have I guarded well through years of bitter strife:
I've raised a daughter. . . miles away—she knows not of my life.
Oh spare her this—her mother's shame. I pray that God may save
That child of mine from men and wine; or send her to her grave.

         *   *   *   *

The Architect of Sun and Earth in wisdom drew His plan:
Each shrub He placed where knew He best—then crowned His
    work with man.
Like a stunted pine on a wind-whipped shore stands a woman
    lewd and lorn,
She stands alone. . . on barren stone, in the wind of human
    scorn.

THE MYSTERY OF MOLLY McGINN

It was down in the Railroad Bar Room of a roaring boomer
    town
That Forty-Mile Jack, the hogger, was quaffing his liquor
    down;
The fire in the old round blazer burned red with a cheery glow,
While Three-Finger Slim, the brakeman, shot craps with the
    bar-keep, Joe.
When into the warmth and carousing came a man, out of God
    knows where,
With the hang-down look and the doleful gaze of a convict sent
    to the chair.

"Well I'll be damned!" said Forty-Mile Jack, "if it ain't old Dan
    McGinn,
Who fired for me on the D. and R. G. in the days of the
    link-and-pin.
You look, by God! like a homeless dog, that's been left in the
    cold to die!
So, just as you are, come on up to the bar . . . Hey, Joe, slide us
    over the rye.
That's better, old pal; now tell us what seems to be on your
    mind."
So, with two rounds more, we listened, while his story of grief he
    defined:

"Well, boys, I guess I'm a rotter and I've fostered a life of sin;
You'd never guess this broken-down wreck had ever a
      bread-winner been.
Yet, once I was head of a household. . .a wife and a daughter I
      had,
But a man that's born to a life of lust will go from the best to the
      bad.
It was down in a town in Wyoming. . .a wife, and a child, and a
      home:
And a truer woman was never born, but the fire in my blood had
      to roam.

The childish prattle of children and the joys of a cottage small,
That glows with the love of a woman, will a normal man
      enthrall.
And it did; for a while I was happy—I thought I'd the world by
      the horns,
But the sweetest joys, like a rose-bud, you will find festooned
      with thorns.
Not thorns that will jag in the finger, but pangs that will stab at
      the heart,
For once a man starts foolin' around, tis then his troubles will
      start.

"It happened one night I met Rita (while the wife sat at home
      with the kid),
And for loving, this dame was a dilly, you can bet that we both
      blew the lid.
Like a cow that's been pastured in clover is never content to eat
      hay. . .
It's about the same with a married man—once sampled he'll
      wander away.
But the love for my daughter, Molly, who'd a cute little mark on
      her thigh,
Curbed the wanderlust pulse in my blood stream; but the wings
      of lust must fly.

"Now the wife wouldn't stand for two-timin', so a note read, I'm
    leaving you, Dan!'
And oddly she blew with a gambler, who left her to die in
    Cheyenne.
This rumour I heard from a boomer, after Rita and I went away
To a frontier town in the Badlands, where hair-trigger justice
    held sway:
But Rita was wife to another, who was faster than me on the
    draw,
Which ended romance with my Rita. . . See here at my
    bullet-creased jaw.

"Well, the years that followed after were roaming, carousing and
    lust,
Sometimes plenty of money, sometimes hungry and bust;
Often battered and bleeding from many a bar-room fight;
But always the same old story: women like ships in the night.
Then I often thought of my daughter. . . just a child, when she'd
    kissed me good-bye,
And I wondered if she had the fire in her blood—was a rotter,
    the same as I.

"But Life, like the sand in an hour glass, sifts the good and the
    bad in a pile,
With the good deeds buried and covered, by the worst ones,
    bitter as bile—
Bitter as worm-eaten driftwood—sordid—disgusting—depraved!
And now I will tell why the streets of Hell with the sins of lust
    are paved:
Why a man his life would sacrifice to forget, or to start life
    again. . .
Just to capture a lived-lost moment, and avert such remorse and
    disdain.

"One night on my drunken carousing, in a den of evil repute,
Where the oldest profession is fostered by the whim of the
    masculine brute:

It was there I met a young woman whose charms plucked the
    strings of my heart.
I was thrilled, yet somehow I wondered why Virtue and she had
    to part.
Then flashed to my mind recollections of a face such as hers,
    long ago;
Ere the Devil's spell from the depths of Hell set the fires of
    Passion aglow.

"But Passion and Lust are the offspring of Eden's beguiling snake,
And Lust is the fruit of Passion, as the raisin is fruit of the grape.
That serpent-born instinct within me, though steeped in a
    cauldron of flame,
Envisaged this girl as an angel—removed from her calling of
    shame.
Then, feasting my eyes on her beauty, I saw . . . but I wished I
    could die!
For the girl of my fanciful vision had a cute little mark on her
    thigh.

        *   *   *   *

Oh! what a flood of resentment now pounded the walls of my
    soul!
To drown in its depths, my one cherished dream: that to such
    she might never enroll.
But apples don't spring from an acorn; nor lilies bloom forth
    from a weed;
It's plain that the law of Nature bears each of its kind from its
    seed.
. . . Don't judge her too harshly; have mercy—judge me; I'm a
    thousandfold worse:
If she veered from the pathway of Virtue, she inherits that
    Eden-born curse.

"That's all. Now my story is ended. Straight whiskey I'll have
    and be going,
I'm headed east on a hot-shot freight, I can hear that old whistle
    a-blowing."

"Life, like the sand in an hour glass,
sifts the good and the bad in a pile."

. . . He was gone! We stood there dumbfounded, digesting his
    tale of disdain.
Next morning we learned that old Dan McGinn had died 'neath
    the wheels of a train.
Had died? Yes, some say suicide: so strangely doth Life sift her
    sand,
For in death was an age-yellowed picture of an innocent child in
    his hand.

LOUIE BORDEAU

From de woods of Quebec come one Louie Bordeau,
Who was come from de Eas' w'ere you log in de snow,
W'ere de reevers you drive, put de logs on de sleigh,
At de horse crack de whip, and she pull d'em away:
On de sleigh-road, at night, w'ere you sprinkle watair,
An' she freezes up tight from de frost in de air.
But de logging out Wes', she is all diff-er-ent
An' Louie Bordeau to one logging camp went.

Now de foreman of camp, he is one tough felloe,
An' he raise too much Hell wi' dis Louie Bordeau;
But she's all diff-er-ent from de woods of Quebec,
An' de foreman call Louie one pain in de neck:
"Buck de tree into logs wi' de beeg bucking-saw,
You frog-eating felloe from Eas' Canadaw!"
But de saw, she is beeg, and one handle she's gone.
All day he is try—but he's nevair buck one.

Dees foreman, he's mad at dees li'l Frenchman,
He is all feegure out for to geeve heem de can.
But de boat, she is late an' de hooker he's mad,
An' for one chokair-man, he is ver' mooch glad;
De punk blow de wheesle—de main-line, she's tight,
An' dat man from Quebec he is stan' in de bight,
She flip from de stump, where dat main-line she rub,

94

So dat poor li'l Frenchman get plenty of troub'.
In de boonk house at night Louie's write one lettair
To dat Mor'eal town (his Marie she is dere);
In de lettair he say: "Dees is funny countree,
Where de logger is monkey an' climb up de tree.
In de summer he work, in de winter go down
An' spen' all he's dollair on girl in de town;
But if Louie learn how for dees logger to be,
He will save up he's dollair an' sen' for Marie."

But de boys in de camp t'ink dis Louie is fool—
He have learn for to log in de boys' Sunday school.
He can run on de log like de frighten' tom-cat,
Or jomp tru' de hole like de Northern muskrat;
He can sweem like de feesh—wi' de peave he's fine,
But he nevair have learn for to splicing de line.
He is worse in de worl' for de beeg logging show,
An' so every one laugh at dees Louie Bordeau.

*   *   *   *

Mon Dieu! How de t'under she's splitting de sky;
De flash from de lightning, de t'under's ally
Is bursting de cloud, an' de rain she is come,
'Till she soun' on de roof lak' de fas' kettle drum.
De reever she rise—an' she's changing her course,
'Till she dance in de rapeed lak' jomping white horse,
An' de log in de watair lak toot'pick she's floating,
She's a fan' on de shore; but no tam' for de boating.

Den dere hearing a cry from de san'-spit, across—
Dat foreman's small boy, on de raf' he is los'!
An' de raf', wi' de boy to de rapeed she's turning,
Where de watair she's white, an' de whorl-pool she's
          churning.
De beeg western loggers—de row boat, dey jomp,
Butcome back to de shore an' dey stan' on de stump:
Dey are scare for dat reever, dere stan'in' aroun'—
De mudder she cry dat her sma' boy be drown.

95

Den jos' lak de shot dat come out from de gun,
You swear dees Bordeau on de watair is run:
He's crossing dat watair lak boat in de stran'
On' de sma' leetle log wi' de pike pole in han'—
Some tam' you don' see heem, he's bob up an' down,
De peopl' on de shore t'ink dees Louie is drown;
But he jomp on de raf', an' he pick up dat keed—
In de spray an' de foam he is shoot de rapeed.

Pre'y soon on de shore is one frighten' youngstair,
Who is wet to de skin from de frot'ing watair.
De mudder geeve kees to dat li'l Frenchman,
W'ile de foreman he's busy a-shaking he's han'.
De beeg western logger dat stan' on de shore
Don' t'ink dat dees Louie is fool any more.
An' de foreman decree, "For such man we have room,
Here's de man we are wanting to work on de boom."
       *   *   *   *
Dere's a shake shingle shantee way down by de shore,
Where de flower of de morning is climb 'roun' de door.
In de sun, on de clothes-line is many diepair,
An' de song from de woman she's filling de air.
She's de happy's woman in all Canadaw,
An' her husban' on Sunday is drink whisky-blanc.
Should you ask for de name of dees husban' felloe,
Jos' knock on de door an' ask Madame Bordeau.

THE WRECKING OF THE "BEAVER"

Now, this is the tale of the BEAVER, *that was wrecked where the mad
     tides rip,
Though I wasn' there, it's true, I swear—read ye the tale of that ship:*

In that Western town, where the Twin Peaks frown, and the
     mountains spring out of the sea,
Was the Sunshine Saloon (that was run by McGoon) where the
     gang were drinking it free;
And loggers and miners and men of the sea together were
     drinking a toast
To favorite women, across the line, who lived on the Barbary
     Coast.
When through a trapdoor that was cut in the floor, and into the
     roaring saloon,
Came a crew of men you won't see again if you travel from here
     to the moon;
For this was the crew of the *Beaver*, that ship of historical fame,
That sailed 'round the Horn before we were born, to flagship the
     fur-trading game.

This seafaring lot got drunk as a sot, with the skipper as drunk as
     the rest,
He was making the boast he'd sailed up the coast with the
     barmaid on board as his guest,
When a wizened old gent, like a corpse from the grave, toddled
     over and stood on the floor—
He looked like a soul that had come from the hole of Satan's
     infernal roar.
"A story," said he, "this is going to be, that'll stand your hair on
     end.
Now I'm telling you I was one of the crew of the *Beaver's*
     mechanical trend.

97

I was there on the day the foam and the spray caressingly
    welcomed her prow,
They'd launched that ship from a Blackwell slip and I sailed
    away on her bow.

"A sturdier craft has ne'er sailed the sea, a vessel so stalwart and
    fleet;
She'd a thirty-foot beam . . . was powered with steam; her keel
    was a hundred odd feet.
And aloft on her decks she sported five guns—had a crew of
    twenty-six men;
Her engines were wrought at Bolton and Watt, with a working
    pressure of ten.
In eighteen hundred and thirty-five her first engineer was
    McGluke;
A Scotsman was he, yet he hated the sea—the sight of the deep
    made him puke.
In his queer Scottish way to the captain he'd say, 'If I die on this
    cold ocean wave,
One thing I desire is cremation by fire, but never a watery grave.'

"One day in May, in the cold Hudson's Bay, McGluke was as
    sick as a dog:
A North-Easter blew, and the captain and crew were plugging
    old Mac full of grog.
As he breathed his last to that icy blast his dying word was the
    boast:
'If you bury me in that icy sea, I'll haunt this ship with my ghost.'
But the captain was full of traditional bull and McGluke in a
    canvas was bound . . .
With a naval salute, o'er the rail went McGluke, and the
    bubbles burst all 'round.
In the dead of night 'twas the eeriest sight that ever a human has
    spied;
For there on the beam, in a cloud of steam, the ghost of
    McGluke sat and cried."

"It seemed to creak and infernally speak of a grave in a restless
    sea;
Its vengeance avowed for each of the crowd, and the one who
    queered a last plea.
The captain died, and over the side went straight to that locker
    below,
And Davie Jones, curator of bones, has the lot all stacked in a
    row.
That paddle-wheel ship made many a trip through arctic and
    tropical scene.
With the ghost of Mac, sat there on the back, bobbing up and
    down on the beam.
Such is my tale," said the grizzled old gent. "It's as true as the
    Book of Our Lord,
So watch for the ghost as you sail up the coast, you can bet that
    it's still on board."

Then the piebald McGoon set up drinks for the room, for the
    Beaver was sailing that night,
And down through the door that was there in the floor the crew
    disappeared out of sight.
The last to go from that booze-fighting show was Marchant, the
    master of ship;
He'd said *au revoir* to the beer-slinging maid, and left with a kiss
    from her lip.
. . . July twenty-sixth, on the midnight hour, in eighteen
    eighty-eight—
With a fond farewell on the old ship's bell they sailed through
    the Lion's Gate:
But alas, their hoard of liquor on board wouldn't last the loggers
    a day;
And the boys were bound he'd turn the ship 'round or they'd toss
    him into the bay.

With the fear of death and a curse on his breath, he swung hard
    over to port;
And she rolled and tossed, like a soul that was lost in a
    purgatorial court.

Then, a rending crash and a shuddering smash! She floundered
    on Prospect Point.
They were thrown on the floor, but they clambered ashore and
    back to that booze-possessed joint.
McGoon stood agog, like a goggling frog, with his eyes popping
    out of his head,
When up through the hole, like a creeping mole—the crew! He
    thought they were dead!
It must be their ghosts, and McGluke's ancient boasts, as it
    bobbed up and down on the beam,
Had scuttled the ship and ended their trip; well, that is the way
    it would seem.

Such was the wreck of the BEAVER *of fame, and such is the story they tell;*
Though a grave in the deep to that ship never came—may the ghost of
    McGluke rest in Hell.

THE WATCHMAN'S DREAM OF CHRISTMAS

Now this is the song that the watchman sang
In the camp of the Northern Spruce,
One Christmas Eve, in his lonely shack—
A night when a blizzard broke loose;
While the breakers roared on the rockbound shore,
And the gulls from the sea came forth,
And the snowflakes fell on the logged-off ground,
As a north wind whipped Queen Charlotte Sound,
As it lashed from the Frigid North:

The old camp feels deserted, 'cuz the boys have all gone down;
They've left with noise and shouting on the Christmas boat for
town.
Now the silent snow is falling, and the landscape's turning white,
I'm the only soul that's left in camp—guess I'll bank the fires
tonight.

So it's Christmas Day tomorrow—how it brings back memories
dear
Of my loved ones. . . long departed, I can hear their voices clear.
I can hear my youngster's laughter as we draped the tinseled
bough;
Guess I'll lay me down and rest awhile (felt queer. . . but I'm
better now).
Ah, well—as the Good Book puts it: He giveth and taketh away,

And they that are born of a woman but blossom forth for a day.
Now it's Christmas Eve . . . but I'm lonely, and I'm old and
    weary, too,
So in memory's eye tonight I'll spend, loved ones, my Yule with
    you.

> *Now this is the dream that the watchman dreamed*
>   *In the camp of the Northern Spruce,*
> *As he dozed to sleep, in his lonely shack,*
> *(And a dry old snag swayed, ready to crack)*
>   *That night, when a blizzard broke loose.*

Saw he the face of his loved one, his child clutched close to her
    breast;
Moist were her eyes in their rapture, like an angel awakened
    from rest;
Sweet was her smile and her bearing—tenderly taking his hand,
Bade him to follow and join them again, in that distant and
    faraway land.

The sleeper took heed to her pleading—rolled back were the
    years of his life,
'Til he fancied the past was the present: Christmas Eve in the
    arms of his wife.
Asleep in her crib was their darling, child's faith in the
    Christmas had she:
To wake in the morning, and gleefully find rare treasures placed
    under her tree.

In bliss was the dreamer of rapture secure in his home as of yore;
Heard not the howl of the blizzard, nor the thunder of waves on
    the sore;
But dreamed (in his dream) he was dreaming: He was old and
    alone in the world;
That his darling was gone; that he lived in a camp, by a shore
    where the mad sea hurled:

In a virgin and timber-lush country, where the mountains
      colossal and high,
Flaunted bare fangs to the heavens—in defiance, snarled up at
      the sky;
Where the rivers, unharnessed and bounding, swept down with
      the freshet of Spring;
Where Man in the scheme of Creation seemed but a crawling,
      insidious thing.

The dreamer felt snug in a cabin, as a wind whistled shrill from
      the Sound;
Fancied he heard timber falling, like cannon fire—deep in the
      ground.
That snag by the cabin! It's falling! The roof is all splintered and
      broke!
The shack had caught fire! I'm held in a vice. . . I'm jiggered!
      And then he awoke.

Awoke, from his dreaming of terror, to the dream of his home as
      of yore;
With his darling, secure in their cottage, where little feet
      pattered the floor.
His dream was a dream without ending, to screen from the
      dreamer his fate.
So, he's dreaming still, in a grave on the hill, of the Christmas
      he spent with his mate.

THE WORTHY BED BUG

When just a boy, young Worthington a woodsman tried to be,
But an *inkslinger's* job appealed to him—so he learned
stenography.
A business course he finished, his shorthand knew he well.
When he was hired by a timber firm, whose name I'd best not
tell.

He slept the night in a run-down dive, where the vermin
scampered around,
And he itched and scratched, and rubbed and smacked, like a
flea-bitten, mange-bound hound.
His eyes were red and bloodshot, and he stared like a branded
steer,
Yet he bravely stepped in the office to begin on his business
career.

Oh the dread that is deep in the stomach that virgin morn on a
job,
When everyone watches each little move—and you grope like
you're lost in a mob!
The typewriters sound like machine guns as letters on paper
they pelt,
And the boss peers down the back of your neck. Well, that's
how Worthington felt.

Soon the boss was heard on the buzzer and Worthy jumped up,
    kinda glad.
Said the boss: "Well, son, take a letter." So our hero went in
    with his pad.
The boss was sat in a swivel-chair that creaked like a rusty
    hinge;
And he filled that chair with nothing to spare, like yeast-worked
    dough on a binge.

He cleared his throat, and started in: "In reply to your recent
    letter. . .
Your service is punk; your shingles are junk; by Gad! you will
    have to do better. . ."
Then he stopped and stared at Worthington, while his hand was
    scratching his head.
Worthington's pants were stuck to the chair, and his heart was
    heavy as lead.

Now, the boss's gaze was glued on the desk (that desk with the
    polished gloss),
For a bed bug walked, in a dead-straight line, from Worthy to
    feed on the boss.
'Twas a brown bed bug with a downcast look, and it walked with
    a jitterbug stride,
Like its thought in mind was a damn good feed and a sleep in
    the folds of his hide.

Two men and a bug. . . each matching his wits (and Worthy the
    scaredest of all),
And the bug looked proud as it jittered ahead; but pride runs
    ahead of a fall.
Now the brain-hatched plan of bug nor man won't always run to
    course,
And care-planned joys will often bring grim failure and
    remorse—

For the boss reached out; his fingers flicked, and the bug-hatched
plan was queered.
Which served to prove to our Worthy friend *that a haste-planned
change should be feared.*
Though the boss's scowl was worse than his bite (for a big man's
view is broad),
No more was said; the issue was dead; and our friend . . . he
wasn't outlawed.

But a lesson learned is a treasure earned: now Worthington
holds a good job—
For the self-same firm, he's the prized *P.A., and his job is for
salesmen to snob,
And his bugs he knows from the toe to the nose, just ask him
and you'll see,
For he'll confess he owes success to a bug . . . as the master key.

---

*P.A.—Purchasing Agent.

THE BOILERMAKER'S HEAVEN

When my last hot rivet is driven,
    And my last steam boiler is caulked,
I'll pass from this land of the livin'
    To tell Old Pete how I've worked:
How I've sweated in hellish hot boilers;
    How I've rolled at the sizzling flues;
How I've slaved with the black-gang toilers
    'Til I've melted the soles of my shoes.

At last when my body's cremated,
    And I'm called to that heavenly mat,
If the All Seeing Boss is elated
    By my life, He will order that
I go down below to the Devil;
    To the heat and the smoke for a spell,
To the depths of the lowermost level,
    And repair all the boilers in Hell.

There'll be Jimmie-the-Rat and his brother
    In the grime of those hot *front ends*;
It's a cinch that we'll know one another,
    For there I'll meet all of my friends;
And the Devil will do all the testing—
    See that staybolts are batted-up well,
While in peace and content I'll be resting
    In the nice, cool boilers of Hell.

FAITHFUL UNTO THE END

On the grand Vancouver Island, by the shores of Horseshoe
    Bay,
Is the town they call Chemainus, where they have a famous
    Shay;
And the man who jerks the throttle, as he puts her through her
    tricks,
Was a youngster, shy, when first the Shay came new in nineteen
    six.

He is known as Old Len Cary by the folks around the town,
And the Shay is known as "number six," the engine of renown.
With her Radley Hunter smokestack and a tender full of wood,
She grinds along at ten per hour—and faster if she could.

With her shining black enamel and her jacket polished blue,
Her bell dolled up with Brasso—she looks as good as new;
For her boiler is a wonder—packs five score and eighty pounds,
One hundred less than Cary—they're a pair of going hounds.

But the cab was getting shaky, and the springs low on one side;
With Cary getting stouter—lop-sided she would ride.
So the M.M. had a brain-wave, and a steel cab did he make,
With extra room for Cary—special springs, his weight to take.

It's a sight you don't see often in these modern streamlined
    days;
An old-fashioned locomotive, and a man who loves her ways.
There's a shack beside the roundhouse; when he spots her for
    the night
They both sleep very snugly . . . within each other's sight.

But what will be the outcome as the long years wear away?
Will the six-spot outlive Cary or he outlive his Shay?
Whichever be the first to go will break the other's heart,
So they'd better go together, then they'll never have to part.

L'ENVOI

The old gang sat and talked of bygone days;
　　Of timber claims we'd logged, and distant camps —
Of big machines, and hauls with roaring Shays
　　And the poker games we'd played 'neath coal-oil lamps.
Another round — we filled each glass — and then
Discussed the days that were — when men were men.

Those roaring days when loggers came to town
　　With stagged-off pants and wearing caulk-shod shoes,
When men like Olsen kicked the jail house down,
　　While Eight-Day Wilson pinched the copper's booze.
A rough and fighting band of hardy tramps
Were those who roamed the woods and hit the camps.

To skid-road queens of yesteryear we drank;
　　To taverns now erased with changing times;
A toast to Fortune — punk, or noble rank;
　　To those who'd quit the game for fairer climes;
To those now rich who'd shared adjoining bunks,
While some aspired, but sank again to punks.

The sombre dawn too early killed the night,
　　Each 'rose to part with clasped and shaking hands,
And all agreed some bunkhouse bard should write
　　The songs of men who roam the timbered lands.
These are my songs, though rough as timber, hewn;
Here are my chips of effort roughly strewn.

Topping a standing spar
Photo courtesy Vancouver Public Library

From **BU**

BULL TEAM — 1886

ROADER-DONKEY and SKID ROAD — 1908

RIVER DRIVING

FLUME

TIMBERR

HIGH-LEAD

SHAY LOGGING LOCOMOTIVE

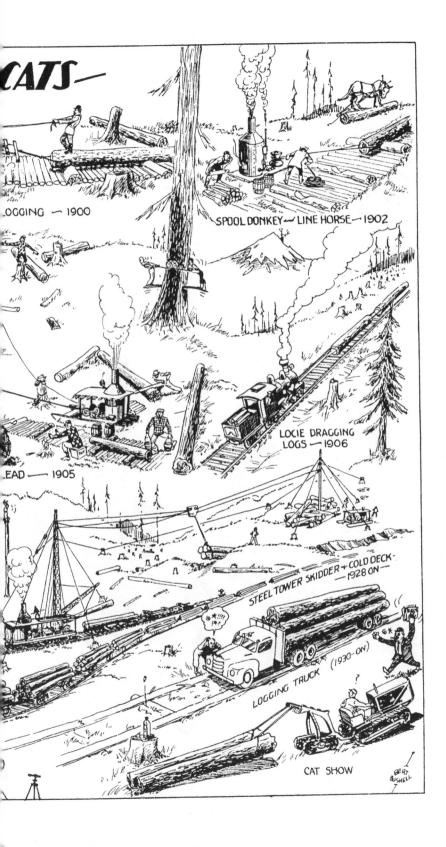

CATS—

LOGGING — 1900

SPOOL DONKEY — LINE HORSE — 1902

LOCIE DRAGGING LOGS — 1906

EAD — 1905

STEEL TOWER SKIDDER + COLD DECK — 1928 ON

LOGGING TRUCK (1930-ON)

CAT SHOW

BERT BUSHELL

Early ground-lead
Photo by Leonard Frank, courtesy Jewish Historical Society of BC

BOOK III:

BUNKHOUSE
BALLADS

WARNING

I have no doubt the critics frown
    When they peruse my verses,
The Censor's sense of rectitude
    Was wrecked on bunkhouse curses.

So let the judge the bookish bards
    Who sing of birds and breezes,
And you and I will sing the songs
    Our heart and fancy pleases.

And so I warn my pious friends
    In case they be offended).
It's for the likes of you and me
    These ballads are intended.

THE CALL OF THE WANDERLUST

Now the winds of spring are rampant, now the distant trails are
  open,
 Now the Spirit of Adventure lures us on —
To the mountains, to the desert, to the Northland, to the ocean.
 When the thaw betrays the grassland, we'll be gone.
He who knows the creak of snowshoes, he who knows the
  desert's heat,
 He who knows the taste of Exploration's brew:
Let him follow in the footsteps of the young men's marching feet,
 Until each one finds the thing he loves to do.

Have you sailed the rolling ocean, have you felt the flying foam,
 With a thousand fathoms deep beneath your bow?
Have you seen the far horizon five thousand leagues from home,
 And wiped the briny spray from off your brow?
Have you heard the combers thunder on a bleak and rocky shore,
 When a landward gale drags anchor to the lea?
Have you fought a stalling engine when it's meant your life — and
  more,
 To keep your ship a mile or more at sea?

Do you know that crystal river where the rapids swirl and
    eddy,
    With the cut-throat leaping anxious to the fly?
Have you hollered to your partner when the trout are browned
    and ready,
    With the fir-bark smoke a-smarting in your eye?
Have you waded in the river? Have you heard your reel
    a-screaming,
    When the rod is bending double to the strain?
Have you sat in placid twilight, in tranquil peace a-dreaming,
    When the Varied Thrush rings out its sweet refrain?

Have you scaled that mighty mountain where the sunset's
    colours blend?
    Have you breathed the mountain's rare and fragrant
    night?
Have you lain in rocky ambush for hours and hours, on end,
    'Til the mountain goat has ranged within your sight?
Have you tracked the rutting bull-moose? Have you met the
    grizzly bear?
    Have you slain the stealthy, green-eyed mountain lion?
Have you camped beneath the starlight, in that great, big
    land—out there,
    And gazed upon the jewels of Orion?

Have you roamed the rolling prairie? Do you know the open
    spaces,
    Where the foot-hills float on mirages of light?
Have you seen the painted canyons? Do you know the lonely
    places,
    And the pungent smell of sagebrush in the night?
And that broad, ranch-house verandah where the cowboys sit
    and croon
    To the harmony of resonant guitars?
Have you rode into the twilight—to a swollen harvest moon
    And promised her a hatful of those stars?

Now the outbound freighter whistles, now the train is steamed
and coaled up,
Now the silver plane wings upward in the blue.
Now the camping kits are loaded, now the charts and marked
and rolled up.
Now we seek the land in which we're overdue.
At Creation's far-flung borders; on the frozen wastes you'll find
us;
The desert's dunes where burning sands are blown;
At the earth's four distant corners we will leave our tracks
behind us,
As we blaze the trails toward the Great Unknown.

THE BALLAD OF THE SOILED SNOWFLAKE

The Madam stood in her parlor when a knock was heard on the door,
Her fairies then gathered around her to display their stock and store.
She peered through the grill in the panel like a panther stalks a deer
And with quick respond to the cute little blond she whispered in her
ear:

"He's fresh in from the jungles, dear, with a great big roll of hay,
So stick right close beside him, and make that sucker pay.
I had my spotter down last night to watch the boats arrive,
And my taxi driver picked him up in an east-end bootleg dive.
He'll be my guest while you get dressed in your finest evening
frock;His tonsils anoint in a cocktail joint, but bank his
roll in your sock.
Offer your charms to lure him—make sure of your feminine wit;
But get his jack, and then come back. It's a fifty-fifty split."

"Hello, dis place!" said Mickey O'Shea, as the Madame ushered
him in.
"I'll quaff me some of your good old rum 'cuz I know you're
drinkin' gin.

Here's to the ladies—God bless 'em, and here's to the
  rum—drink her down;
Skoll! bottoms up; best o'luck; fill the cup, there's plenty more
  liquor in town.
Now, trot out your girls for my choosin' for my flesh is seared
  with the flame
That has burned in man since the world began (O, need I
  mention its name?)"
"Now, dearie," the Madame intruded, "I know you're a-rearin' to
  go,
That roll you pack, of hard-earned jack, is a mighty big wad of
  dough!
Just be advised by one who's wise to the tricks of the Huntress
  Clan:
Steer clear of the harlot, the women in scarlet, she's out to fleece
  you, man.
So let me make you acquainted with the right kind of gal to
  acquire,
She's honest and true and she'll see you through, shake hands
  with Molly Macquire."

"What a woman! My God! What a woman," thought the man
  from the log-jammed streams.
I'd follow her track to Hell and back, she's the girl of my fanciful
  dreams.
. . . I've lain all alone in the darkness of the forest with boughs
  for a bed,
With the towering pines up above me, and the murmuring wind
  overhead—
And I've heard her voice in that stillness, and she's come like a
  nymph ere the dawn,
To soothe my soul with her fondness. With the stars and the
  night she'd be gone.
And always I've fancied I'd seen her in those big, deep pools of
  blue
Where the cataract leaps in the river, I've heard her laughing,
  there, too.

And now, just to think she's beside me—O God, but it's hard to
　　believe. . .
"Come, Honey, let's head for a night club," said the blonde little
　　daughter of Eve.

＊　＊　＊　＊

Ten thousand drums and a big brass band, queer animals, purple
　　and red,
Were climbing the walls with ten pound mauls and a-thumping
　　them down on his head:
A circus of serpents performing in a bathtub full of champagne,
They were long, they were lean, they were purple and green and
　　a-writhing around in his brain.
. . . A woman—a marvel of beauty, with a form like a sculptor's
　　dream,
With rippling laughter in her eyes, like the moon on a mountain
　　stream,
Was calling him close to her bosom, was enticing him to her
　　embrace;
But always her image would vanish and the floor would wallop
　　his face.
Now, was it a horrible nightmare, or the jims from the liquid fire?
Had the Madame not made him acquainted with a girl called
　　Molly Macquire?
He seemed to remember a road-house where the twinkling,
　　bright lights shone.
Then, sudden, he ran through his pockets—his roll—My God! It
　　was gone!!

＊　＊　＊　＊

How cold were the streets of the city, how barren, how friendless
　　and bare.
How lightly the snowflakes fluttered, pure white, on that
　　turbulent air;
How soon were they soiled in the gutter, their emblem of purity
　　stained.
Like the maiden whose visage he'd conjured in the forest where
　　solitude reigned.

He was heading right back to his little log shack on the
    north-bound boat that night.
How he spent the day it was hard to say, yet, he seemed to
    remember a fight.
Battered and bruised and badly used, and nursing a big black eye,
While many a dame of skidroad fame was waving her love good
    bye...
When the steward tapped on his shoulder and beckoned him on
    with a sign:
"If you're Mickey O'Shea, then follow me. You're wanted in
    stateroom nine!"

It was Molly Macquire, his heart's desire, that opened the
    stateroom door,
And she said with a grin, "Come on right in, you're blocking the
    corridor.
You'll think I'm tricky, but listen, Mickey," said the blonde as
    she opened her purse,
"Last night on the spree we saw a J.P. and you took me for better
    or worse.
And here's the whole of your hard-earned roll that you gave me
    to hold for you,
And now I'm your wife you can bet your life I'll always be honest
    and true!"

There's a house in the city that's builded on the sins by the Devil
    ordained,
Where the snowflakes drift in the gutter, their emblem of purity
    stained;
There's a little log shack in the forest where Repentance has kindled a
    light,
And the snowdrifts gleam in the valley, untrodden, untarnished and
    white.

. . . COULD BE!

The typist girl had caught a cold
    And had a runny nose,
She packed around two handkerchiefs
    Somewhere in her clothes—
Was sure she had them on her
    Tucked down in her brassiere,
The more she felt and fussed around,
    She wore a look of fear.

"I'm sure they must be down there,"
    She said, with puzzled frown.
"I hope I haven't lost one—
    It could have fallen down.
I'll put my arm down from the top
    And feel around below;
For where the world it's gone to
    Is what I'd like to know."

The men around the office floor
    Were wondering what was wrong;
They didn't think of *handkerchiefs*
    She fussed around so long.
They watched her preen with interest, keen,
    Until she said, unshaken,
"I'm sure I had *two* when I came—
    But might have been mistaken."

THE CAT-SKINNER'S PRAYER

I've shivered and shook on a Dozer
 I've ranted, and raved, and I've cu'sed.
My kidneys are dislocated
 And I've swallowed ten bushels of dust;
My fingers are broken and bleeding
 From wielding the tools of repair.
O God of Internal Combustion,
 Please answer a cat-skinner's prayer!

Now, I've studied your parts-book Bible
 And here are the things I require:
A pair of unstretchable cat-tracks
 That will never "come off" in the mire;
But the thing that would tickle my fancy,
 When I'm miles from the fuel supply,
Is a tank, for both gas and for diesel,
 Of the type that will never run dry.

Oh, send your toil-worn disciple,
 Who has gobbled and swallowed your smoke,
A heaven-invented fuel pump
 That will fire on every stroke,
A set of perfected injectors
 With guts that will never wear.
O God of Internal Combustion,
 Please answer a cat-skinner's prayer!
Please send me the grease of perfection
 And a change of eternal oil,
Some diamond bearinged cat-rolls
 That will run in abrasive soil,
A final-driving assembly
 With everlasting gears,
And a set of sleeves and pistons
 That will run for a million years.

"O God of Internal Combustion,
Please answer a cat-skinner's prayer!"

Oh send me the lining, immortal,
   For my steering-clutch mechanism,
And a cranking-motor magneto
   With permanent magnetism;
A set of valves and tappets
   At which I will never swear.
Oh God of Internal Combustion,
   Please answer a cat-skinner's prayer!

Great God of the Red-Hot Piston,
   I have worshipped and served you well,
Forsaking the Gods of my fathers,
   Till my soul has been slated for Hell!
If you'll send me the things that I ask for
   I will never work Sundays again;
But I'll worship Internal Combustion
   Forever and ever. Amen.

"THEY'LL DO IT EVERYTIME"

Oh, they rave of Babe and Mabel
When the lines are snarled and kinking,
It is then they give the fancy women snuff,
    But they rave of logs and cable
    In the tavern when they're drinking,
Instead of getting 'round to do their stuff.
    Oh, the air is full of branches,
    And the biggest logs are yarded
When they're drinking with the ladies in the Port.
    But when they eat their lunches,
    Then the logging is discarded
For the king of all, both in- and outdoor, sport.

    When the sunshine makes projection
    Through its dust-strewn shafts of light,
Of the bunkhouse window pattern on the floor,
    And the little flies go zooming
    Like bombers in the night
To land upon the pinups on the door.
    It is then the conversation
    Of the bunkhouse Casanovas
To the giddy heights of fantasy is hurled.
    And they spiel their own ovation
    As the subject passes over
To the universal pastime of the world.

    But get them at a party
    When the womenfolk are handy,
They will promptly start to top and rig a tree.
    It is then our bunkhouse hearty
    Is a logging camp Jim Dandy
Instead of getting Mabel on his knee.
    For the donkeys start a-fogging

And they'll pile the logs around you,
With the price of hemlock rising by the quart;
   But when they *should* be logging
   It is then they get around to
The king of all, both in- and outdoor, sport.

HE'S GOT'ER MADE!

He's donated his boots to the bull-cook and he's thrown his
gloves in the fire;
He's struttin' round camp in his oxfords, dolled up like a country
squire;
He's argued the point in the office on matters of bonus and pay,
And he's all washed up with the outfit, and he'll soon be on his way.
He's said goodbye to the rigger, to the push and his scissor-bill
crew,
And he's paid his regards in the cookhouse to the mixer of
mulligan stew.
Now, he wouldn't call Jesus his uncle, as he lights up a fancy
cigar:
For he's got 'er made and he's headin' fer town on the
southbound *Cassiar*.

He stands on the dock in the darkness till she whistles just ten
hours late,
And he bounds up her ancient gang-plank, while her winches
are juggling freight;
Explains to Paddy the purser, in a world-wise sort o'way,
That he's said good-bye to the jungles. Says Paddy, "The *Hell*
you say!"
In the dining saloon he is puzzled by the spoons with the silvery
gleam—
He reaches across for the sugar, upsetting a jugful of cream.
Now he wishes he'd bunked in the bull-pen (with an ape he's
about on a par),
But he's got 'er made and he's headin' fer town on the
southbound *Cassiar*.

He waves farewell to the mountains as she steams by an "A"
frame show:
No more of yer side-hill gougin', up to yer belly in snow.

He's finished with fallin' an' buckin', with sweatin' and hittin'
  the ball;
No more of yer rotten camp-cookin', he's saying good-bye to it
  all.
He's living on expectations of his glorious days ahead:
He'll get him a long-haired partner, and he'll paint Vancouver
  red,
And he'll never go back to the jungles—to the land of the
  high-topped spar,
For he's got 'er made, and he's headin' fer town on the
  southbound *Cassiar*.

THE BULL PEN BLUES

He's back on the boat for the jungles with his face all bruised
and sore.
He's blown one thousand dollars; now he's back to earn some
more.
It seems he'll never understand the skidroad code of play:
That the only thing they want of him is just that hard-earned
pay.
Oh it's "Thank you, hon, my darling, dear. It's such a lovely
gown."
But it's "Stick him in the Bull Pen, boys," when he's broke and
leaving town.
"He ain't no good; he's just a bum; be sure to treat him rough.
Way down below, between the decks, the Bull Pen's good
enough."

To the finely furnished office in the throbbing heart of town,
Where the typist girls apply their rouge, and the big-shot-brains
sit down—
It was there, while the taxi waited, he explained his precarious
plight:
How someone had stolen his wallet in a bootleg joint—last
night;
How someone had beaten and bruised him, relieved him of all
that he had;
Now, fifty bucks would see him back, he'd catch the boat and be
glad.
"Fifty bucks!" said the tycoon, as he spoke, and his voice was gruff.
"What does *he* want with a stateroom? Why, the Bull Pen's good
enough!"

So, he's down below in the Bull Pen on the surging, bounding
main.
He'll save himself a summer's stake and do it all over again.

And he'll rear and he'll tear on the side-hill or float on the
    booms in the bay;
Or dodge at the holler of, "Timber-r," as the fallers rhythmically
    sway.
And he'll strut on the logs in the forest like a prince endowed
    with a crown.
For he's king in his kingdom of Woodcraft, but a serf to the
    harlots of town.
And they'll fawn to his whims with their favors just as long as
    he's buying them booze;
Then ship him off back to the jungles to the tune of the Bull Pen
    Blues.

B.C. HIBALL

I've toted logs in the woods of Maine,
Worked on a boom in the West Coast rain,
Topped a tree on a Redwood-show,
And I've piled pine logs in Idaho;
But a hiball show I'd yet to see
'Til I hit the woods around B.C.;
And, brother ape, I drink a toast
To the way they log on the B.C. Coast.

In town, at Hicks, my eyes explored
The jobs displayed on the hiring-board.
One caught my eye—a lone survivor;
In letters of chalk, it said, "Truckdriver."
"Ye can cross that off," I said—"and quick.
At drivin' a truck I'm mighty slick!
I'm the best gear-stripper this side of Hell . . .
McGinty's the name." And I waved farewell.

I hit the camp as a logger would,
Sampled the grub and the same was good.
Sat on my bunk with satisfaction
And doffed my city clothes for action.
It was still pitch dark when I heard the shout:
"Roll up, you bums, or else roll out;
In the cedar-swamp it's breaking day,
And around *this* joint we make her pay."

Then the foreman said, with a scowling frown:
"The *dudes* they ship up here from town
Are graduates of a dumbo class,
Right off the farm, and as green as grass!"
His voice fair reeked with authority

"She was gathering speed in spite of Hell!!"

As he wheeled on his heel and said to me:
"Go, herd that truck of the Diesel breed
And let's see some of ye'r Yankee speed."

Ye can talk of yer mammoth trucks of fame,
But this one put them all to shame.
She was air equipped, with a torque retarder,
With gauges enough for a slack-line-yarder.
She'd twelve-foot bunks and a streamlined snout.
So I warmed her up and headed out;
That diesel purred like a cougar-cat
As I clipped a mile in a minute, flat.

Then I hit the grade and the rip-wrap plank,
So I gives the gear-shift knob a yank:
She rubbed the guard as the rear-end slewed
(But kept on gaining altitude).
Up—up she roared, as on we went,
Up a grade of twenty-two percent.
'Til, dead ahead, I could plainly see
The lashing lines of a full-rigged tree.

There, a diesel-yarder did her stuff
From a cold-deck pile on a big rock bluff.
And the echoes resounded with never a pause
From the diesel-electric falling-saws;
While beneath the tree, on a pre-load rig,
Was a load of logs—God awful big.
I backed my trailer beneath that load
And I steered the works for the rip-wrap road.

I was doing fine when I hit the grade,
But here's the only mistake I made:
I'd plumb forgot in the bustle and roar
That it froze black frost the night before.
The more I braked, the more she slid,

Then, eighteen tires began to skid!
I hit the guard-rail—hugged it well. . .
She was gathering speed in spite of Hell!
   * * * *
I was dazed but I sat on a cedar chunk
And gazed at a mangled pile of junk.
A pile of junk that was once the truck
From which I'd escaped with Devil's own luck.
I dangled afar from the tangled wreck
To make a long cross-country trek;
And they never found out at the hiball joint
That I caught the boat at a distant point.

And late that night, as I hit the trail,
I could hear an air-horn's mournful wail.
They were yarding logs in the dead of the night,
And falling trees by the pale moonlight.
I could hear the roar of a diesel truck
A-wheelin' logs to the briny chuck:
But the boys maintain on the B.C. Coast
What I really heard was McGinty's ghost.

QUEENIE, THE QUEEN O' HEARTS

Now, speakin' of women—I've been with a few—the sober, the
    good, and the bad.
I've settled to none but I've had my fun wherever was fun to be
    had;
I've learned some tricks from the slick, blond chicks, ah, many's
    the dandy I've seen;
But I learned what I know about women and love from Queenie,
    my Skid-Road Queen.

138

Now, one was a kid from the Prairie; she was green and she
 didn't know how.
I was teaching her love by installment and I would have been
 nursing her now;
But I moved further north to Alaska—got a squaw by the name
 o'Irene,
And I conquered her heart by displaying the art that I'd learned
 from Queenie, the Queen.

And then it was Winnie the waitress—a bundle of love and
 desire,
Her tresses were treated with henna and scorched to the colour
 of fire.
She doubted at first if she'd make me (I was shy and a little bit
 green),
But I cancelled her doubt when she tried, and found out what I'd
 learned from Queenie, the Queen.

Then, Sarah, the minister's daughter: at first she was shy and
 demure,
But I got her one night on the sofa and it didn't take long 'til I
 knew 'er.
She sobbed and she cried like a youngster and babbled how
 naughty we'd been;
She wanted to wed, but I showed her, instead, what I'd learned
 from Queenie, the Queen.

But I met with a feminine joker that was cunning and slick as a
 mink.
She made me go bail for her husband, who was cooling his heels
 in the klink.
She promised her pleasures so freely, and told me to call her
 Delphine;
Though I bought her a fur I could never show *her* what I'd
 learned from Queenie, the Queen.

So Queenie, the Queen, is the queen of the lot, and I found that
    the last was the worst;
For the more you fool 'round and the more that you know, the
    more you'll remember the first.
And each has a *first* he remembers imprinted on memory's
    screen;
And each has a past (though his first be the last) and each has
    his Queenie, the Queen.

ODE TO MY LADY'S EYEBROW

Her brow reflects her every whim:
Whether 'tis me she loves, or him.
If arched, her brow, in lilting laughter,
Tells me a kiss will follow after.
When lowered in a curving line
I wonder if I'm doing fine;
And then, at times, her brow says clearly,
"I love you darling, O so dearly."
Proudly they span those lustrous eyes
When she's amazed in sweet surprise.
If knitted in a gloomy dip
My darling pouts her lower lip,
And then I say good-bye to glee,
"Move over, dog, make room for me."
But soon they arch in proud-flung joy
And say, "I love you, darling boy."

NATURE'S HAND

The work of Nature's awful hand
   Rests in the western clime:
Where rolling plain and mountain high
   Outlive recorded time;
Where swollen sun of a blood-stained hue
   Sinks in the Western Sea,
Those flaming sunsets burned the sky
   Before man came to be.

Those awe-inspiring Rockies
   With spires like giant teeth
Set in the jaw of mountain range
   Where valleys yawn, beneath,
Like tired Creation taking rest,
   The clouds her panting breath;
For Mother Nature's awful hand
   Knows not the pall of Death.

The gnarled and twisted strata
   Of those huge colossal peaks

Reflects Creation's magnitude,
    Of great upheaval speaks.
Where once the stupid dinosaur
    Wallowed in shallow streams
Is now the crest of mountain range—
    Fantastic though it seems.

Those sedimentary sandstones were
    Laid down by ancient streams
Meandering through their peneplains—
    Her plan thus Nature schemes.
What seems complete is just begun,
    She merely sits at rest;
Has changed her whole work over
    For naught can stand her test.

What was the dizzy altitude
    Is now the valley's floor.
In yester-age the solitude—
    Today, Niagara's roar.
She'll change it all in man-made time
    And do it o'er again.
Oh man! her meagre creature here,
    Ye dare to check her rein?

The drenching storms are but her tears,
    The lightning bolt her wand;
And planets in their orbits fare
    As pawns to her respond.
For time and space mean naught to her;
    (The product of man's mind)
Boundless infinitude is She,
    Yet part of all mankind.

Pause yet a moment, mortal man,
    In your brief sojourn here,
Let wait your burning treasure lust,

Your superstitious fear—
Your greed for power to rule the world:
Remember mortal flesh
Is but a part of Nature's plan,
Her die can cast afresh.

Think not that man of earth-bound greed
Can comprehend her flaws,
Nor do her bidding, yet, awhile,
Your conscience knows her laws.
For she doth rule her universe
With hand like iron rod;
Remember, Mother Nature is
But just the hand of God.

THE VENGEANCE OF THE HAIDA GODS

There's a dark-eyed maiden waiting where the Northern Sun
    sweeps low,
In her sealskin robes she's standing where the ocean breezes
    blow.
And at night she stands there dreaming of her loved one, far
    away,
When the Haida Moon is gleaming on the ice floes—'cross the
    bay.
        On the shores of Old Skedan,
          There she met her sailor man,
        And her dark eyes flashed their greeting,
          And her love-life thus began:
        "Bring me back my reckless lover,
          Bring him back ere yet ye can;
        Bring me back my wandering sailor
        To the shores of Old Skedan."

But the sailor kept on roaming on a far and distant strand,
And the Haida maiden waited in her Northern tribal land.
Now a broken-hearted maiden sleeps in peace for evermore,
'Neath the towering trees, snow-laden, on her native Haida
    shore.
        Journey back to Old Skedan,
          O you faithless sailor man.
        Place the cross of faith upon her—
          On her grave ere yet ye can.
        Journey back to Old Skedan,
          O you reckless sailor man,
        Ere the Haida Gods wreak vengeance
        From the shores of Old Skedan.

"And the Haida Maiden waited
in her Northern tribal land."

THE HEART OF A REDWOOD

Perhaps, in this secluded spot,
Some valiant warrior might have fought
His mortal foe with flint-hewn knife;
Each grappling, tussling for his life,
Then, drinking deep, the gushing blood
Oozed in the sod its crimson flood.
The valiant warrior here lay still;
The ebon raven gorged his fill;
. . . And ages passed. . .
Yet, here where once a warrior bled,
This giant tree, a seedling, fed,
Staining its heart that blood-like red. . .
The murmuring wind bespeaks his woes:
This might have been. Who knows? Who knows?

146

CLIMAX COURAGEOUS

It was out on a haywire, homeguard show
Where the ground was rough and the crew was slow;
Where a rusty, crooked railroad track
Wound out of camp past the rigger's shack.
Within that shack, in wedded bond,
Resided the rigger's wife—a blonde—
Who was wont to wave with a glint in her eye
At the engineer as he thundered by.
His ancient Climax, worn with years,
Would clash and clang its hypoid gears,
Shiver and shake and hump its back
As it wheeled those cars up the crooked track.

Now Dusty Dan, the engineer,
Was fond of women, wine, and beer,
But a fondness, still, excelled all these:
He'd tinker and toy on his bended knees
Down underneath, in the filth and stench,
And tighten up nuts with a monkey-wrench.
The Climax coughed like a horse with the heaves
Shedding its nuts like autumn leaves,
Till scattered along that right-o'-way
Full many a bolt and pinion lay.
But at last one day, with her valve-stem slack,
She stalled in front of the rigger's shack.

147

Out piles Dan, as the Old Girl stalls,
Doffs his cap and his overalls,
And in he goes, as large as life,
To monkey-wrench for the rigger's wife.
The panting Climax, standing by,
Was shedding grease on the railroad tie.
And every day when the line was clear
Her air pump churned the atmosphere:
Till the ties in front of the rigger's shack
Were covered and coated with gear-grease black.
(And the Super learned from the office clerks
That the chief was fixing her water works.)

But out in the woods where the cables hum
The main-line had bust right close to the drum,
An empty landing, bleak and bare,
Greeted the train crew's dismal stare.
The loaders slept beside the grade,
While empty tongs in circles swayed
Above the empty cars, below,
Where loaded logs had ought to go.
The weary engineer leaned out
And hearkened to the brakeman's shout:
"We'll wait for loads—so spot yer fire
And monkey wrench to yer heart's desire."

The breathing pulse of the air pump dies,
While Dusty Dan his art applies
Deep in the guts of her vital points,
A-wrenching the nuts of her flexible joints.
Like a monster wakes from a fitful dream
Her pistons throbbed the pulse of steam!
And Dusty Dan rolled down the bank
As he missed the grabs on her water tank.
Away she rolls, down the crooked track,
Shedding her nuts with her brake-shoes slack,
And gathering speed, with the switches lined,
She left the gaping crew behind.

As thunder rolls on a mountain ridge
The Climax crossed the Bear Creek bridge,
Her flanges screaming upon the rail
As she steered her course down the mountain trail.
While far to the rear in hot pursuit
Galloped the crew—with the Super to boot.
The brakeman said, as he cursed his luck,
"She'll pile in the weeds or she'll plunge in the chuck."
But an awful silence strains their ears,
No more is heard the clash of gears.
With her smoking wheels still on the track
She was stalled in front of the rigger's shack.

THE POET AND THE RAVEN

Low the summer sun was sinking, still I pondered, dreaming,
    thinking—
Thinking of the soul's departing when it leaves this world of woe.
In that sunshine's level gleaming, might have been that I was
    dreaming
On that bare and barren hill-top, far above the sea, below;
On that wild, deserted mountain where the phantom breezes
    blow.

Faint, at first, I heard a rasping like a soul in terror gasping,
Like an organ-pipe, discordant, with a reedy, rasping note.
And it said: "Oh, fellow mortal, ponder not on things immortal
Past that veiled and deathly portal where the vampire spirits
    float—
Past the rosy realms of reason where the imps of Pluto gloat.

"Ere Time's grim and grizzled reaper sent my soul to Hades'
    keeper
A mortal man I wandered in the realms where men abide.
Ah, I recollect, so clearly, how I lived and loved too dearly,
A girl more fair than Venus ere I crossed the Veiled Divide—
A girl whose smile still lingers like the sun at eventide.

"Ringing still, her loving laughter through Time's Corridors,
    thereafter
Haunts me—taunts this soul in terror with an all-consuming
    shame.
Yet, how well this soul, in sadness, recollects the thrills, the
    gladness,
That was ours in love's mild madness, to be sealed in Heaven's
    Name—
To be sealed before the altar 'neath the flickering candles' flame.

"For a raven sat beside me,
perched upon a shattered tree."

"Like the soothing intonation of a minstrel orchestration
Stirs the soul of him who listens—grips him in a rapturous
     spell. . .
Then, before his eyes there flashes wrongs that sting like
     leathern lashes
When a brazen cymbal clashes its shivering, clangorous knell.
Thus love's interlude was ended with that one I loved too well.

"Low a gloomy cloud descended ere love's interlude had ended,
Dark the nebulous intruder crossed my star-flung Milky Way.
Oh, a devil was the potter when he formed that rougish rotter,
For with lover's lies he got her focused as his spell-bound prey,
And she yielded to his pleadings and King Pluto held his sway.

"Seemed it, now, possessed within me was a demon, deemed to
     win me
From the paths of Truth and Reason to the grasping clutch of
     crime.
All my aspirations shrinking I betook myself to drinking,
Still my brooding brain kept thinking of that stolen love,
     sublime;
And the demon's voice would whisper, 'Coward, kill him, waste
     no time.'

"Thus possessed and evil-passioned, straight, an arrow's shaft I
     fashioned,
With its plume a raven's feather and its point a lethal dart.
Deep into the twilight wending: shadow unto shadow blending;
Evil unto evil sending, when I bade that shaft depart:
But the raven's feather veered it and it pierced my lover's heart!

"Thus Love's Goddess was offended, so my mortal life was
     ended,
And Death's grim and grizzled reaper took my soul from mortal
     clay."
With concluding words it stated: "We are spirits doomed and fated,

Here, on earth, reincarnated, punished souls we wing our way;
Doomed as ravens in the forest where as men we lived our day."

*   *   *   *

Low the summer sun was sinking, there I pondered, wondering,
      thinking:
Was that voice the phantom echo of some lost mythology?
Little wonder that I ponder on that mystic dream out yonder,
Where the ghostly shadows wander in black-plumed fantasy;
For a Raven sat beside me perched upon a shattered tree.

Note: a legend of the Northwest says that every raven in the forest is the soul of
a departed woodsman.

THE MAN FROM CHEYENNE

Our stakes were made—two days to go:
When the boat arrived, into town we'd blow;
And we'd sit in a lobby, so snug, in town
A watchin' the snow come tumblin' down.

The wintry sky was dismal and bleak
As the rigging came back like a silver streak
In a sleeting rain that would soon be snow
We were soaked to the skin from head to toe;
While the white exhaust in a phantom breeze
Seemed to drift clean through the stumps and the trees.
Yet, the Greenhorn Kid would jump in and collar
His Bardon Bell ere the hooker could holler.

In at camp that night, on the window pane,
The steam from our socks tickled down like rain;
With our Stanfield suits all hung there drying,
And a howling wind through the rafters sighing:
Said the Greenhorn Kid, "Now look here, pards.
I'll go you gents to a game of cards."
With a wink, says Slim, "We'll trim this joker;
We'll fatten our stakes in a game of poker.

Spread the tablecloth of a blanket, grey,
And we'll shuffle the pack and start in to play."

When the deck was cut and we dealt around
The flutter of cards was the only sound.
Low stakes at the start (and a nod on the sly)
"Let him win three hands, then milk him dry.
We'll play this game to its finest point
And we'll spend his dough in a plush-lined joint.
Women and wine, and a parlour, warm,
And we'll laugh at the kid in the winter's storm."

Soon the pot was raised and the game broke loose
While the fallers stood, jowls full o' snoose,
Around in a ring, intently still,
Like a wolf pack watching the lead-wolf kill.
To the kid, said Slim, "You, skin the cat."
I opened the pot and we both sat pat . . .
With the kid all out, the stakes sky-high,
An ace in the hole and we milked him dry.

Then the Greenhorn Kid, like he held an ace,
Put a chip on the cloth just to hold his place.
To the bull-cook's shack, in the rain, he scoots,
And he bummed ten bucks on his new caulked boots.
But a different kid was he who came
Back to the shack to continue the game.
" . . . The code of the game is the law of the pack:
Stick around for the kill and you might win back."
It was thus he expounded nonsensical rot
As he opened the play with a ten in the pot.

His eyes glowed bright but his face grew bland
As he dealt that pack with an agile hand . . .
He raised the pot—then I saw him flinch!
I watched my mate and it looked like a cinch
For a bob-tail flush, or four-of-a-kind,

So I threw in my cheque, all duly signed.
A murmur arose. . . I felt like a heel.
Snuff colored Gods! could that man deal!
For the kid lay down and he stood ace-high,
Raked in the pot and he milked *us* dry.

* * * *

In the brush next morn at the crack of dawn,
In a yard of snow with our stakes all gone,
We thought of the kid, all dressed up fine,
A-heading for town where the bright lights shine.
Would he think of us in the winter's storm
With his feet propped up, in a lobby, warm?
Well, I think he did; 'cause he nailed this note
On our bunkhouse door ere he caught the boat:
"Look me up sometime if you're 'round Cheyenne,
And learn how to deal, from a gamblin' man."

THE CALL OF SPRING

The skylines sweep o'er the side-hills, steep—'cross the bowl of
    the azure sky,
And the echoes roll from knoll to knoll as the swishing crosscuts
    fly;
The toppling trees sing melodies that are music sweet to the ear,
And the waters roar on the canyon floor, but, O, so crystal clear,
It's the only life removed from the strife of a world gone raving
    mad.
So when axes ring at the call of Spring, it's a thrill and my heart
    feels glad.

O, to breath the air of the Great-Out-There, when the
    spring-flushed torrents race,
Where things are real and a man can feel the beat of the rain on
    his face,
As he breasts the gale on the open trail in that great, big
    Outdoor Land,
When the woods turn green by a wand, unseen, in the grip of
    Nature's hand.

O, I want to go where the breezes blow and the white waves hurl
on the shore,
And the swallows return—it is then that I yearn to be back in
the woods once more.

O, to hear the frogs in that land of logs ring out their spring-time
tune,
As the starlight shines through the stalwart pines, and I see the
pale spring moon.
When the breeze is stilled, and the east is filled with the blush of
the new-born day,
The morning mist will roll and twist as it moves out, down the
bay.
While the coffee brews I'll lace my shoes and watch those colors
change
As the rising sun puts gold upon the snow-capped mountain
range.

So remove me, afar, from the clang and the jar of your city's
ceaseless roar,
And set me down miles, miles from a town on a pathless
woodland shore—
For I've had enough of your big town stuff until now my belly's
full:
I'm tired of your streets, of your two-bit cheats with their
well-phrased, well-slung bull.
And I'm sick in the crop of your restaurant slop, of your mobs,
and your city's smoke.
When the robins sing at the Call of Spring, I'll be glad to go
back . . . 'cause I'm broke.

THE BALLAD OF THE PENCIL PUSHER

He's a mile above the average and a little bit high-hat—
Quite a bit above the boys that hit the camps.
Educated—highly polished—he's a real aristocrat.
And he won't associate with lowly tramps.
  He treats us with disdain,
  Cuz he figures we're insane
When we pound upon his counter our demands:
  Lets us rave and lets us holler;
  Lets us burn beneath the collar;
Lets us wince, and lets us squirm at his commands.

He was born to rule the rabble with a sharp, sarcastic tongue.
And he'll never miss a chance to slap them down.
But he takes it, and he likes it, when the Super flings the dung;
Or when he phones the Big Shots in the town.
  Then he'll sweetly acquiesce,
  So his answer's always—"Yes!"
And he'll yes, and yes, and yes, for all his worth.
  If the boss turns on the laughter
  He will quickly follow after,
And show his golden molars as in mirth.

Though the boss's jokes are corny and he's heard them all before,
He is never rude enough to interfere.
When the boss walks in the office, he is tickled to the core,
He will drop a little tale into his ear:
  Sweetly crooning, "Yes, J.B.,
  It's the truth, you look and see.
Those trucks are only hauling half-a-load."
  It is thus he sows dissension
  With venomous intention.
And another man goes walking down the road.

159

He is seething with ambition, and his underhand desire
Is to put the superintendent on the run.
He's the brains around our outfit (though he cannot hire and fire)
But he loves to tell us how it should be done.
　　　There is nothing he don't know,
　　　For he thinks he runs the show,
And without his help we cannot get along.
　　　He's discovered we all hate him,
　　　And he knows we underrate him;
But he thinks he's right, and all the world is wrong.

THE TALE OF THE DYING TRAMP

He was one of the clan of the open road
   That carried his home on his back.
He had no friends nor fixed abode,
   Just an old, brown duffle-sack;

A picture or two of a girl he knew,
   An ancient shaving kit,
Some rumpled shirts and a few ripe socks
   As strong as a brakeman's mitt.

We'd carried him into the first-aid shack,
   His caulked boots lay on the floor,
And we laid him down on the flat of his back.
   Never to rise no more.

He gazed in the fading light of day,
   With a sad and wistful eye.
As his lips grew numb I heard him say,
   "My time has come to die."

"I was just a bum of the cinder trail,
   But now I'm a dying tramp,
Who's found that the road of the glittering rail
   Ends in a lumber camp.

"Yet I was the pride of a college dean
   In the days of my flaming youth,
The pride of a mother's joy, serene,
   Who sought the truest truth.

"I sought Ambition's brightest star
   To which I set my helm,
Till I was the Chief—the mighty Czar
   Of a great industrial realm.

"But cold Ambition's beacon fire
    Too soon will lose its shine
For Passion's glow and heart's desire,
    And a woman's lips, divine.

"A woman smiled; the Devil grinned,
    And Fate's hand rolled the dice.
And so, serenely, on I sinned
    In a fool's own paradise.

"I found she played a two-time part
    And panic seized my brain,
I drilled her lover through the heart,
    Then grabbed a west-bound train.

"A wanted man from year to year
    Beneath a boundless sky . . .
Till Fate decreed I wander here,
    Into this camp to die.

"You ask my name? Perhaps you've heard . . .
    . . . God! Help me — get — my breath . . ."
But ere he spoke another word
    His lips were sealed in death.

L'ENVOI

We've sung the songs of virile men
  Who roam the outdoor land,
Where Comradeship and Brotherhood
  Unite our restless band.
God knows we've faltered now and then,
  But God will understand.

And now, farewell, the hills grow dim,
  The sun's last vagrant ray
Upon the mountain's ragged peaks
  Reflects the parting day;
And darkness clothes the canyon's rim —
  I lay my pen away.

Western Hemlock

Photo by Leonard Frank, courtesy Jewish Historical Society of BC

BOOK IV:

RHYMES
OF A
HAYWIRE
HOOKER

WARNING

If when you read the rhymes herein
And think they are depraved,
Remember that the streets of Hell
With good intent are paved.

Remember, too, that in a zoo,
The monkeys let you feed 'em;
And books are just about the same,
Regarding folks that read 'em.

THE HI-BALLERS

Oh, they came in droves upon us,
   On the good ship, *Cassiar*,
To spread the Hi-ball Gospel
   In those northern lands afar.
They brought their hi-ball cousins
   Who brought their next-of-kin,
And woe betide the other guy
   Who tried to chisel in—
Who tried to steal their thunder—
   With contempt and a cunning knack
They fawned upon his overtures,
   Then knifed him in the back.
They forged their chain around them.
   To unite each hi-ball gink,
Then hired a hi-ball blacksmith
   To forge the closing link.
And they showed the northern woodsman
   How to really duck the fog
When they'd spent ten million dollars
   And they never hauled a log.

KLONDIKE MIKE

I'm Klondike Mike Mahoney from that ice-ribbed land of gold
King of the dog-team mushers of whom strange tales are told.
By the lore of that Northland's legend they"cremated Sam
    McGee":
But the man who mushed that frozen corpse I'm a-telling you
    boys was me.
I lugged a grand piano 'cross the summit of Chilcoot Pass
On that gold-mad trail of ninety-eight, when the mercury froze
    in the glass.
But my saddest misadventure—and I loathe to think of the
    thing—
Was down in the town of Dawson in a bar-room boxing ring.

Now I was the Boss of the Arctic in a rough-and-tumble way,
Blazing uncharted northland trails—mushing a dog-team sleigh,
Hardboiled, tough and tow-headed, I toiled through the long,
    long nights,
Trekking that awful stillness by the blaze of the Northern Lights;
Charting new trails by the compass—sleeping in robes 'neath the
    snow,
While the huskies howled out their anguish to the night that
    was sixty below.
It was then that I'd get 'round to dreamin' of my youth and the
    things that I did,
When I sparred in the ring with my buddy, who was known as
    the Michigan Kid.

Strange how my mind would go ramblin' to our days in the
    Michigan woods
When me and the Kid drove the rivers, on the logs, in the
    roaring floods.
And at night how we'd spar 'round the shanty in the blaze of the
    campfire's light,

When I was the champion high-kicker and the Kid was a devil
    to fight.
He was fast as a panther in action when it springs in defence of
    its young,
And his punch was as sharp and decisive as the jaws of a steel
    trap sprung;
His physique, then, the acme of manhood—a glorious thing to
    behold. . .
Then I'd suddenly wake from my dreaming to the night, and the
    snow and the cold.

Well, I toted my gold out to Skagway—packed the news of the
    strike outside.
Watched men arrive by the thousands—gold-crazed—and the
    weaklings died.
Saw them sucked down in the rapids, frozen to death on the
    trails,
Helped them build boats for the Yukon and burn them again for
    the nails;
Men writing cheques for a million—wild-eyed and weirdly
    insane;
Father fought son for advantage, brother slew brother for gain.
'Twas the melting-pot of Creation, where the Devil proved each
    by his worth,
And the dross of the melt was the harlot with the oldest
    profession on earth.

I staked me a claim on Dominion, hit pay-dirt galore at the start;
But was broke and in debt in a fortnight, for a fool and his
    money soon part.
It was then that I went into training—got in shape for a
    twelve-round bout
With a scrapper they'd brought up from Frisco—a champion
    beyond any doubt.
Came the night of the fight with the bruiser and the miners
    came straggling in,
Each with his gold into Dawson to indulge in his own kind of sin.

The floor was fresh-scattered with sawdust, the ropes were
    inspected and tight,
The music-box died when the ropes had been tried and the
    betting was placed on the fight.

Have you ever been faced with a moment that you seemed to
    have lived once before?
When you gaze in the face of Creation to foretell what your fate
    has in store?
It was thus for the bat of an eyelash I saw my opponent out cold,
And his muscles were ravished and palsied—a pitiful sight to
    behold. . .
Then the bell!—and we jumped to the centre-of this trance I was
    finished and rid.
We clinched and I saw my opponent—My God!—'twas the
    Michigan Kid!
"Look, Kid," I said low, in a whisper, as we clinched and sparred
    for the show,
"You're finished—washed up—I'm your buddy, I could finish you
    off in a blow."

"Put 'em up and let's fight," was the answer, as he punched me a
    right in the mug.
Came a voice booming up from the miners: "Mop the floor with
    the big Irish lug!"
We sparred and we clinched and we parried 'til he seemed like a
    man in a spell.
Round Eight: he was led to his corner just saved by the grace of
    the bell!
Round Ten: and the Kid like a wildcat, but with scarcely the
    strength of a child,
With the miners a-cheerin' and whoopin' and his punches all
    crazy and wild,
I put in a jab just to hold him—then his eyes rolled back in his
    head.
He crumpled and fell and was silent and the Michigan Kid lay
    dead.

There's a grave on the Dome back of Dawson, where the mighty
    Yukon flows;
There's a little white cross by the trail side, in the land of endless
    snows;
There's a cross in my heart that I carry for a pal I had to fight,
And a prayer in my soul of atonement to the God of Eternal
    Right.

WHEN SNOOSE WAS KING

It was up on the Charlotte Islands where we logged the mighty
    spruce,
Where the fallers all quit falling 'cause the camp ran out of snoose;
Ran out of snoose completely, there wasn't a pinch to be had!
And a craving pain in Ole's brain was driving the Big Swede mad.

"Ay tank dis camp iss haywire an ay tell youse guys da truth:
Ay've vorked in Minnesota an ay've logged around Duluth,
But of all da haywire outfits—ay ban tank aye should vamoose,
Ay'me sick like a dog an a man don't log vitout a schew of
    snoose!"

The woods were full of timber, the outfit full of fight,
The Swedes plumb full of anger with nor more snoose in sight.
The Superintendent ranted and phoned the brains in town:
"It ain't no use, we're out of snoose, and the outfit's all shut down."

In Tycoon's Roost the wires were scorched with cursing and
    abuse,
For the woods were full of timber, but the camp was out of
    snoose.
The tugs all lay at anchor with not a log to tow
And the skidder standing idle in a million dollar show!

Then the Brass Hat in the office got to wracking at his brain
And phoned the Superintendent he'd send an aeroplane
To fly some Copenhagen to camp that very night,
And a bomber plane went roaring on a northbound mercy flight.

Over mountain, hill and valley did those throbbing motors roar
With the precious cargo sitting by the pilot on the floor.
As she landed on the water just as graceful as a goose,
The Big Swede bellowed at her, "You ban got a schew of snoose?"

THESE THINGS REMIND ME

Daisies festooned with dewdrops, sparkling in the morning
      sunshine,
Petals of apple blossoms fluttering in the wind of Spring,
Those long, cool evenings of June in the moonlight,
Alder trees flashing by as speed I down a country lane,
The constellation of Orion rising before dawn dimly kindles the
      eastern horizon.

These things are indeed dear memories:
When I remember the purple glow on a mountain lake after
      sunset,
The godly timbers reaching their arms towards the copper sky.
Driving through a park when the fresh-fallen snow muffles the
      passing traffic's sound
And the bending boughs silently slip their burdens of snow to
      the ground;
But the most precious of my memories is the memory of that
      night when I first found you.

SO MOTE IT BE

When Death's darkness overpowers me
    And my life's tide ebbs in flight,
Let your radiance light my pathway
    Onward through the Stygian night.
Let my memory softly linger,
    Let my soul in solace dream
Of the days we spent together
    When we journeyed on life's stream.

Let me sleep the sleep unending
    Where the wild rose petals fall,
Where the boughs bend low and whisper,
    Where the grass is cool and tall,
Where your presence gently lingers
    In a spot that we have known;
Where I've kissed your slender fingers
    Let me sleep beneath the stone.

Let me know that life's fulfillment
    Was complete because of you
Let me thank the Gods that placed you
    In my life the journey through;
Let me sleep with no regretting
    In some cool sequestered dell;
Light my pathway through the darkness
    When I bid this life farewell.

THE TRUCK BUG

You've heard of the hemlock looper
And the hungry budworm, too.
You've heard of the deforestation
These parasites can do;
But of all the deadly insects
Down to its last descendant
Is the deadly"Truck Bug"when it stings
A logging superintendent.

When once he's stung he'll rant and rave
Of trucks and stinking rubber,
And grades of thirty-six percent
Without a brake or snubber.
He'll suffer grand delusions
Of finely graded roads,
Of rooting railroad down the hill
And hauling ponderous loads.

He dreams of locomotives—
All melted down for junk,
The hogger—thin and scrawny—
A lowly whistle punk.
I don't know yet the antidote
As I pen this little rhyme,
But railroad men please pray to God
They'll waken up in time!

THAT WHISTLE IN THE NIGHT

Oh diesel queen of the glittering rail,
　Pride of the streamlined train,
Your throbbing pistons rule the grade
　Where once was Steam's Domain.
The iron horse has spent his day,
　Now fades his thundering might;
But diesel, diesel save for me
　That whistle in the night.

Silence forever—if you must—
　The roar of steam and fire.
Let soulless men be satisfied
　With the growl of a diesel flier.
The clanking rod and roaring stack
　Forever fades from sight;
But diesel, diesel save for me
　That whistle in the night.

Oh, let me hear that plaintive wail
　Across the lonely plains,
Or hear the snow-clad peaks fling back
　The voice of thundering trains.
Then in my soul there stirs a peace
　That tells me all is right;
So diesel, diesel save for me
　That whistle in the night.

THE CAMPS OF THE HOLY GHOST

When the world's last timber is yarded
  And the donkeys are laid aside,
When the hooker has met his Creator,
  And the last, lone chokerman died.
We will rest and Lord we will need it!
  Lie down for a century or two
Till the Bull of the Universe hollers
  And calls for another crew.

And those who are hired by the Master
  Will be loggers of West Coast fame,
Who will wrestle those feather-weight chokers
  To log off that heavenly claim;
And they'll dine in a wonderful cookhouse
  On hotcakes one foot thick,
And eat for a year at a sitting,
  And no one will ever be sick.

The donkeys will always be popping
  On six hundred pounds of steam,
And the spars will be rigged by an angel
  Inspired by some heavenly scheme.
So lead on to that wonderful timber
  Away from this dreary coast,
To the land of perpetual sunshine
  In the camps of the Holy Ghost.

THE LAST HAIDA RAID

The Chief of the tribes had spoken and his
    was the voice of command:
Five hundred strong to your war canoes
    and plunder the Southern Land!
Five summers long we've let them breed and
    bask in their southern sun,
Slaughter the sons and their fathers, (but watch
    for the White Man's gun)
Make captive their virgins and children
    and bring them north to be slaves
The thongs of your sculptured bow sprits
    shall be draped with scalps of their braves:

The blood-red disc of the rising sun now
    climbed from a blood-red sea,
Till the towering spruce and the snow-clad
    peaks were as red as blood could be.
The heathen Gods cried out for blood when
    the council feast was done,
And the war canoes of the Haida raid were
    lost in the rising sun.

Ten rising suns had run their course ere
    yet that stalwart band
Of Haida braves had gained the strait that
    guards the Southern Land.
And each man knew red blood would flow
    ere yet the moon would wane.
The Southern Land was rich with spoil the
    Northern Isles would gain!

Where rapids swirl through Skukum Chuck and
    lurking dangers ride
They passed by stealth the outer guard who

watched the racing tide,
And gained the Southlands' sheltered sea—still
further south they bore,
While distant camp fires flared in peace
along the sheltered shore.

        *   *   *   *

The Raven Chieftain raised his voice above
the war-lust cheers:
"At dawn Camosun's Camp will feel the
might of Northern spears,
Ere yet tomorrow's sun descends in yonder
western sea
The Southland's mighty tribe will bow to
Haida tyranny."

Ere yet they struck five hundred strong,
the Northern Chieftain cried:
"The Raven and the Eagle tribes are fighting
side by side.
Today your Southland blood will pay, and we
our vengeance swear
For Southern slaughter to our tribe, whose
emblem was the bear."

Then answered back Camosun's Chief:— "Our
God, the Bird of Thunder,
Has placed a curse on Northern tribes who
journey south to plunder,
And this, the curse, O Northern men, our God
of Thunder gives:—
"Their flesh shall rot upon the bone while
yet each victim lives!"

Authors' note:—In 1945 I interviewed Captain Billy Brown, a Haida Chief who
then lived at Juskatla, Queen Charlotte Islands, regarding the authenticity of
the "Haida raid" stories handed down from father to son over the centuries. As
nothing factual could be established I thought it best to leave the conclusion of
the above poem to the reader's imagination.

ASHES AND DUST

Last night the moonline through your hair
A halo formed above your brow
Your love was mine, alone, to share—
That love is dust and ashes now.

Can love endure from year to year
Chafings its bonds—a gossamer thread—
When broken brings the burning tear
And hearts' regret when love is dead?

Memory, the arch that spans the mind,
Returns you to my souls' delight,
Warmly I feel your arms entwined
But wake to find the empty night.

Ah, fondly though I recollect
the ecstasy of Love's embrace
Your burning lips—Desire's effect
When I gazed down upon your face

The dust and ashes from that fire
Kindled in hope, consumed with pains,
Once fed the flame of Love's desire.
Perchance the spark of love remains!

That spark if fanned with gentle care
Perhaps will flare to flame again.
Will love come back our lives to share
Or deeper sear our souls with pain?

IN NONE BUT THE LONELY HEART

I am alone in the midst of many
Alone, not by the dictates of an empty feeling within my heart
Because I cannot see you.
Around me, on every side, are many people —
Human people, that live and breathe, and have
    their being;

I scan the many anxious faces, hoping
That by some unforeseen turn of circumstances
    yours might be amongst the many.
But I search in vain . . .
Until I find myself delving deeper and deeper
    into the archives of memory . . .
Searching and hoping,
And when I see your comforting countenance
    smiling down upon me
I am then no longer alone,
For I find I have you with me — within my
    heart.

LOVE ME FOREVER

Ah, life is sweet and life is good when
    I behold your form,
Your eyes, your lips, your smile, your arms
    embraced so close and warm;
Your finger tips upon my brow my darkest
    fears allay;
But, O, my dear, I'm lonely now that you
    are far away.

I'm lonely for a heart that lives for one
    sweet hour divine,
A heart whose roots and tendrils cling
    around this heart of mine.
I'm lonely for the voice that gave a promise,
    truly given;
I'm lonely for the arms and lips that carried
    me to heaven.

O, passing time is but a farce, for hearken
    what I say:—
Tomorrow dawns and is today, and soon is
    yesterday;
And all the future joys we sought when
    realized and gone
Are rolled in one with yesterday as time
    goes rolling on.

And so my love, the day will dawn when binding
    ties we'll sever,
And then as time goes rolling on we'll
    be as one forever,
And future bards, not yet conceived, may raise
    their hue and cry
When fate has thus its pattern weaved our
    love shall never die.

COMMUNION OF SOULS

The night, empty as my arms, closes in around me,
The distant lights linger upon the water and are at last—
Lost in that utter void of loneliness, now that I am here
    alone.
Familiar trees gaze down upon me,
Seeming to sense the emptiness that clutches my soul.
Our stars shine down from the firmament of heaven
But they have no message for me:
For to be alone and to be lonesome in a place that holds
    such dear memories.
Fills my soul with loneliness.

Oh, my darling, dearer than life itself,
Surely you must sense that I am here to bask in your presence,
Here in our dear spot to be alone with the memory of you;
Here, to reflect upon the ecstasy that has been ours,
Here to commune with the Fates that brought us together,
Here to reflect, in utter despair, and think of you and you
    alone.
Ah, fortunate is he who can be alone with the memory of the
        one he loved
For now, each wave and tree that rustles brings a message to my
        ear,
A message from the one of my hearts' dearest pain.
Hearken to the message they bring:—
Distance, time and space shall be erased,
And in this hallowed spot you shall again be as one
    with her.

RETURN, O MY LOVE

My life seems empty like a shell cast
    up from an ocean of turmoil
There to lie and bleach in the sun meaningless,
    empty and without purpose.
O, glorious sun which once kindled a halo
    above the form of your angelic brow,
Why do you taunt me with the remembrance
    of the golden days we have known together?
Together in the warm possession of each other's
    close embrace,
Pregnant with the throbbing ecstasy of passion,
We tempted fate and obeyed the undefilable bidding
    of our creator.
Obeyed—that our likeness should live on when we,
    ourselves are part of that great oblivion
To which all flesh is heir when time has called
    its number,
Return then, soul of my life, return from where
    thy creator forbids thee to dwell,
And cast this empty shell back into the
    turbulent ocean of life.

CANADIAN NOSTALGIA

Lonely men and lonely women
On the vast and far-flung prairie
Hear the distant steam train's whistle
Linger in the frosty night;
And its sound is reassurance
That another human being
Sends a greeting o'er the vastness
To a distant kindred soul

When the lofty mountain's grandeur
To the brim is filled with silence
Drifts the voice of locomotives
From a world far out, beyond,
Then the lonely mountain hermit
Snug within his moss-chinked cabin
Tosses on his pine-twig mattress
As he slumbers and he dreams

Way down east in Nova Scotia
Where the split-rail fences wander
And the scowling, dark Atlantic
Wrestles with the rock-bound shore
There the train sounds perk and saucy
As it winds through woods and meadows
Blending, blending with the landscape
And the settler's way of life

In the nation's great metropolis
Where the teeming millions trample
Where the lights are artificial,
And the stars eclipsed in shame
Then the friendly steam train's calling
To a warning cry triumphant
As it rattles to the station
At the panting journey's end

185

A LOGGER'S DICTIONARY

A

"A" frame show: a tower built in the form of the letter "A", 150 feet high, rigged up on a float, a show is logged off with this rig.

ape (usually "tame-ape"): a rigging man.

arbor: the shaft on which a circular saw is fastened.

ass: the back end of anything.

B

bag boom: logs in water surrounded by boom sticks in circle.

Bardon-bell: Bardon choker hook of manganese steel.

bicycle: a skyline carriage used in logging.

"big holed the air": put air brake in emergency.

bight: to be inside the angle of a line or block.

bitch: a tough anything (a bitch of a day); skidder hook.

blew the lid: to get out with gusto; to quit in a hurry.

blue butt: a large fir butt, usually pitchy.

board hole: a hole cut by fallers in a stump for spring boards.

bob-tail-flush: a hand of cards in poker.

boom: logs rafted in water ready to tow.

boom chain: a chain used in booms.

boom stick: a long, thin log used crossways in booming logs.

bone yard: place for worn-out machines.

boxing gloves: counterweights on a Climax locomotive.

brains: the headmen, bosses, owners, etc.

"brawl": the noise made by a torrent of water (not a logger's term).

brow log: a log to protect log cars at spar tree.

brush: in amongst the felled timber.

bucked: cut off in the woods with a saw.

bucker: a man who cuts logs when felled in the woods.

buckskin: a log from which bark has peeled off (in the spring).

buffer beam: cross timber on pilot of a locomotive.

bull: conversation as a pastime.

bull of the woods: the superintendent, foreman, etc.

bull block: a large open-mouthed pulley block.

bull bucker: the boss of the fallers and buckers.

bull car: a big flat car to move donkeys on.

bull cook: man whop puts in wood, makes beds, etc., in camp.

bull moose: a large anything.

bull pen: second class steerage on a northern boat.

bull wheel: a large-toothed gear wheel.

bunk: a rude form of bed; anything but the truth; in reference to equipment, the chairs on the truck or car upon which logs are carried.

bunk house: the residence of anything but a happily married man.

butt rigging: short lines between chokers and main line.

C

cant: a piece of lumber from head rig (not edged).

carriage (in mill): car which logs are sawed up on.

186

cat: a caterpillar tractor.
cat-rolls: the rolls upon which cat tracks operate.
cat-skinner: a caterpillar tractor operator.
cat-tracks: the tread of a cat tractor.
caulk: a spike in a logger's boot.
caulked boots: spiked boots for walking on logs.
chaser: the unhook man at the spar-tree.
cherry-picker: machine for picking up lost logs on a railway.
"chicken-crap show": miserable outfit.
chin-whiskered: poor show; haywire;lousy.
choker: steel cable with hook end to put on logs.
chokerman: man who puts on chokers (setting chokers).
chuck: Chinook word for salt water; the sea; food.
chunk: a log not bucked off at both ends; usually left in the woods.
churn butted: swollen butt of log.
cinder-trail: a large main line railroad.
claim: timbered country surveyed to be logged by a company.
clears: timber or lumber with no knots.
Climax: a breed of geared locomotive.
cold-deck: a pile of logs to be yarded to home tree.
complaining: something which a hooker does a lot of.
compound: a double geared donkey engine.
conifer: a cone bearing tree.
conkey: a tree infested with a parasite fungus (rotten).
crock: a bottle of liquor.
cross cuts: cross cut saws for cutting logs.
crown: the top branches of a standing tree.
cruise: to measure up and estimate standing timber.
crummie: a closed boxcar for hauling persons.
cull: a log lower than the lowest grade.
cupola: a lookout on a box car, or speeder.
cut: a railroad excavation.

D

dame: a female person aged from 9 to 90.
dangle: to move fast.
deuce (the deuce): number 2 locomotive.
diapasonal: sound like lowest note of pipe organ.
diesel-electric falling saws: power saws for sawing and bucking, using diesel-electric power from a portable central generator, 180 cycle A.C. current.
diesel yarder: diesel powered yarding donkey.
dipper: part of a gas shovel.
dive: a place not so good.
dog: a hinged hook on a log carriage in a mill.
dolphin: several piles driven together in the water.
dolly: a roller for timber.
dome: part of a locomotive boiler.
donkey: a logging engine with drums.
donkey puncher: donkey engineer.
doughnut hook: a hook with a ring to keep it shut.
dozer: bulldozer.

droop: stoop-shouldered person.
drum: a part of a donkey.
duplex: a loading donkey with double engines.
dutchman: a block on a line to keep logs off track, or to divert course of logs.

E

eagle eye: sharp eye; loco engineer.
edger: edging saw machine in a saw mill.
"eleven by seventeen": a donkey whose cylinder is 11 x 17 inches.
eye: a loop splice in end of cable.

F

fair lead: rollers in donkey to spool the lines.
fake: a gas donkey.
fall block: a block below carriage in skylining.
falling and bucking: falling trees and cutting them up into logs.
felled: fallen (applied to timber and snags only).
fill: a railway embankment.
fir: a coniferous tree of the west coast.
flicker: a woodpecker, bird of the northwest.
flunkey: a table waiter or a dishwasher.
flyer: a skyline machine (special system).
four-of-a-kind: a hand of cards in poker.
friction: a donkey clutch.
friction-pins: part of clutch on donkey.
fog: steam.
fore and aft: road of logs laid lengthways to travel.]
fusee: a burning railway signal.

G

galloping goose: a locomotive that runs with galloping motion.
gandy-dancer: a section hand (tie tamper).
gear-stripper: truck driver, sometimes "gear jammer."
gillagahike: a machine for rolling skyline.
girth seam: seam of boiler parallel to axis of same.
goat: a rig-up donkey.
good-head: a good fellow to work with.
guard rail: fender log on a plank road.
"guthammer": dinner gong.
guy: a guy wire to hold spar-tree vertical.
guy: a male person aged from 9 to 90.
gyppo: a small log contractor (poor, haywire).

H

hang-up: fouled turn (see turn).
haulback: line which pulls rigging back in yarding.
hay burner: a horse.
haywire: inclined to be not up to standard (broken).
head block: front high cross member of a donkey sled.
headrig: complete outfit for sawing logs in mill.
headlight: main front light of a locomotive, etc.
headsaw: main rip saw for logs in sawmill.
head-tree: spar-tree next to the railway.

188

heart: centre growth rings of a tree.
heel-line: line for tightening skyline.
hi-ball: go ahead fast, start, fast-outfit, fast.
high-lead: system of logging using spar-tree.
Hindu: short cable to fasten lines (skidder).
hiring board: blackboard upon which jobs are written in a hiring office.
hitting-the-ball: working very fast.
hog-back: mound between two rivers.
hogger: locomotive engineer (hog=locomotive).
holt: the application of a hitch of rigging.
home guard: a man who works for the same company and never quits his job.
hooker: hooktender; boss of yarding crew.
hooter: male blue grouse from March to July 1st.
husk: frame work for head saw in mill.
hypoid gears: bevel driving gears whose pinion shaft centre is above (or below) the shaft centre of the driven gear.

I

inkslinger: time-keeper or office man.

J

jack: money; a loading block hung on a guy line.
jack-pot: a hell of a mess.
jagger: sharp strands on worn cable.
jewelry: rigging, hooks, knobs, etc.
jill poke: a prop, which when motion is started will cause an object to move in another direction; also a log unloading device.
J.P.: Justice of the Peace.
jug: jail.
jungle: a name for the logging camps and woods.

K

kettle: a boiler.
kickback: a timber fouled in edger thrown back by saws.
king pin: part of a log car; the main person.
King Pluto: Ancient Greek god of the underworld.
kink: a twist in a cable.
knit: to splice.
knoll: a rounded timbered ridge.
knuckle: part of a coupler on a locie or car.

L

lap: term in valve setting (donkey).
lead: a block in line (to hang a block).
line: "line" is said when enough slack has been pulled out by hand, also the name for any rope.
loaders: the men who load logs onto cars or trucks.
locie: a logging locomotive, also known as "a hog."
log dump: end of railroad where logs are put in water.
luff: an application of blocks and lines.

M

machine: usually a donkey.

mainline: the main hauling line in yarding.
main-line: the main railway.
marlin spike: splicing spikes.
mill: sawmill; an old locomotive.
Molly Hogan: a link made of wire strands; or an eye.
mug up: cup of coffee, not at mealtime.
mule: corner belt drive in a mill.

N

nigger: vertical steam log-turner in a mill.
North Bend System: a system of skyline logging.
nose: front of a machine (or front of anything).
nose bag show: had to pack a lunch bucket to work.
notch: a groove in a stump for a guy line.

O

open face: a wide drum donkey.

P

pannicky: always in trouble, or excitable.
parbuckle: a holt on log causing same to roll sideways.
peeler: log fit for veneer making.
pencil pusher: time-keeper.
peneplain (geological): a region reduced almost to a plain by the long-continued normal erosion of a land surface; as distinguished from a plain produced by the attack of waves along a coast.
pension: an easy job.
percolate: to make a machine run well.
P.F. man: man who rides skidroad "pig."
pig: sled used in skidroad to bring hooks back.
pile: log driven vertically in ground; pile of logs.
pile driver: machine for driving piles (not surgical).
pinion: smaller of two gears on a donkey.
pot: steam logging donkey (locie).
powder-monkey: man who uses powder in woods.
pre-load-rig: in truck logging logs are loaded upon a hydraulically raised and lowered dummy truck and when loaded the real truck is backed under and the load transferred to the truck.
"pull the pin": to quit the job and go to town.
punk (whistle punk): signal man on yarding crew.
purchase: a good steady pull (using blocks).

Q

queered: spoiled;refused a plea;spoiled the plan.
quirk: an artful trick.

R

raft (Davis raft): invented by Davis at Port Renfrew, B.C.; a boom of logs capable of being towed in heavy seas, bound up with cables.
"raise hell": to do anything in a boisterous manner.
rat: a small person; a no-good person;an informer.
reach: an extension between two log cars.
receding line: line which takes back bicycle in skylining.

reefer: a refrigerator box car.

rigging: lines, hooks, etc. (on the rigging-yarding crew).

rigger (high rigger): man who tops trees and rigs same.

rigger (skidder): head man on a skidder show.

rip-wrap: cable spiked crossways on a plank road for traction.

rob: to steal parts of one machine for another.

roll: a holt to cause log to roll when pulled on.

S

sash: frame of a gangsaw.

scaler: man who measures and calculates logs.

school marm: a forked log or tree.

scissor-bill: a stupid person.

section crew: a railroad track repair man.

sedimentary (geological): rock formed by sediment deposited by water or wind.

set: toothside clearance in a saw.

setter: man who sets logs for sawyer in a mill.

setting ("a setting"): a piece of country to be logged off to one spar tree.

shackle: a clevice.

shake: a hand split cedar shingle.

"shanty queen": logger's wife living in a shack in camp.

shay: a geared locomotive; sidewinder; stemwinder.

shear log: a log to guide others past a stump.

show: conditions governing output of logs.

side (a side): a complete yarding and loading, falling and bucking show and crew.

side-hill-gouging: this term is derived from the mythical animal known as a side-hill-gouger, whose right front and back legs are very short while the left-side legs are very long. This animal is said to frequent side hills and can only travel in one direction, consequently it runs around the mountain in one direction only.

side-swipe: to hit sideways.

side winder: a tree knocked sideways by another tree; or a smaller fork of a tree going straight up parallel to the trunk.

siwashed: line running around anything but a block.

sizer: a timber planing machine in a mill.

skid road: road on which logs are dragged.

skidder: a skyline system for rough ground; a donkey engine special for this system.

"skidroad": street in town which loggers frequent.

skin-the-cat: to deal the cards.

skyline: 1¾ to 2¼ inch steel cable, three thousand feet long, to haul logs through the air in rough country; skidder.

slack-line-yarder: a ponderous, complicated skyline donkey engine.

slash: logged-off country.

sled: sled on which donkey sits.

snipe: to cut end of a log so it won't dig.

snub: to hold back with cable.

soup: superintendent.

spar-tree: tree topped and rigged in high lead system.

speeder: a rail car motor driven on railway.

spot (2 spot): number two locomotive; a locie number.

squaw-hitch: manner of fastening a log with a choker.

stake: wages saved up to spend on a spree.
stand: a good "stand" of timber.
stanfield suits: long woolly underwear.
strap: a steel cable with two eyes to go on a stump or spar-tree.
straw line: small line to pull haulback.
stump: what is left in the ground when tree is felled.
suckhole: a tale packer to the boss.
"sugar pine": a large California tree.
super: superintendent.
swedish fiddle: a bucking saw.

T

tag: another, older name for butt rigging.
tail-holt: back fastening for haulback (or snub line).
tame ape: a real logger.
tangent: a straight piece of railroad.
tank: tender of a locomotive or donkey.
ten-by-twelve: cylinder of donkey 10 by 12 inches.
thread: to pass lines through blocks.
tight-line: signal three-two, to pick rigging straight up in air (yarding).
timber: logs and trees fit to be logged.
Timber-r-r-r!: signal call, "Keep clear, tree is going to fall."
tit: the throttle of a donkey (or loco).
tongs: tongs used to load logs on cars.
"top a tree": rigger climbs and cuts off top.
topog: timber cruiser's topography map.
transfer block: a block used in skyline rigging.
transfer line: line to move skyline.
transit: surveying instrument (gun).
tree ("in at the tree"): "inside" the guylines of spartree.
turn: in yarding, the logs hauled in one trip.
twin-hooks: two hooks fastened together with a link.
"two-inch skid": flat spot on a flat car wheel (condemned at 2).
tycoon: an industrial potentate or a big boss logger.

U

undercut: the notch cut determining which way a tree will fall.
unit: a combined yarding and loading donkey on railway wheels.

V

virgin forest: forest not yet opened up for logging.

W

wedge: a wedge used in tree falling and bucking.
whistle: a signal (on a whistle) in yarding logs.
widow-maker: a loose limb hanging high in a tree.
wrench: to repair a machine.

Y

"Y": the letter y (chamber in "k" and "h" triple valve).
Y: a track for turning a locomotive around.
yarding: hauling logs from the stump into a pile at the track.